How to be a
COMPLETE

BAS ARD

I dedicate this book to myself (because I'm Bloody Great!)

First published in Great Britain
in 1986 by Virgin Books,
a division of W. H. Allen & Co Plc,
44 Hill Street, London W1X 8LB

Reprinted 1988 (twice)
Reprinted 1989
Copyright © 1986 by Adrian
Edmondson, Mark Leigh and
Mike Lepine

ISBN 0 86369 182 X

Printed and bound
in Great Britain by
Scotprint Ltd, Musselburgh

Typeset by Witwell Ltd, Liverpool

Designed by Sue Rawkins for
The Bloomsbury Group

BASTARD CONTENTS

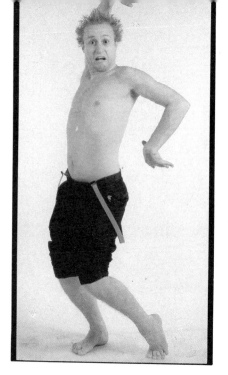

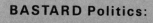

BASTARD Politics:

HOW TO BE
INCREDIBLY
IDEOLOGICALLY
UNSOUND

CONSERVATIVE

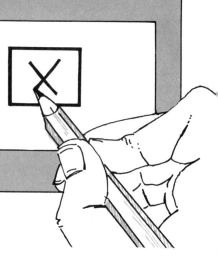

Foreword
by a
*Famous
BASTARD

Effendi, You have truly shown the divine wisdom of Allah in purchasing this literary jewel. I am grateful indeed for the opportunity to let my feelings be known within one of the greatest scriptures in the west.

Adrian Edmondson is a truly noble man, with the endowment of a camel. If it were not for Adrian, I would probably still be washing up in a Kebab House behind Piccadilly Circus. For it was Adrian who first said to me "Hey, why don't you piss off back to Libya and start a revolution — that'd be a laugh wouldn't it?" It was Adrian who suggested that I wear military clothing as opposed to a pair of onion bhajees sellotaped to my chest, which was the original style I adopted.

Indeed it was even he who advised me to select America as the "Great Satan" instead of Luxembourg.

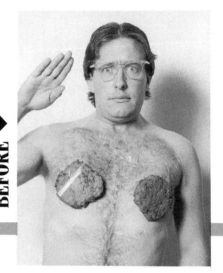

Many are the times we have spent beneath Allah's glorious firmament, watching the setting sun, as beautiful as any pearl within the navel of an Arabian Princess, and playing "Ker-Plunk". On one such occasion I remember Adrian sipping his anorak (arak?), turning to me and saying:

"Listen Gavin, you arsehole. I've got this fantastic idea for a book about being a complete bastard, and I want you to write the foreword."

Of course, I would do anything to show my untold gratitude. Adrian is like a veritable son to me, and looks on my beloved wife Debbie and my dear children Tracey and Duane as if they were his own family. So here it is —

The Foreword
≈

What a great book, it's much better
than the Koran.
(With better pictures too).
LOVE

Gavin

G. Gadaffy (Colonel)

Introduction
by a
Complete
BASTARD

Dear Reader,

As you may already know — I am a complete bastard. If you don't believe me just turn to the back cover of this book. . . . Yes **£3.95!** You've been done! I despair that any of you will ever make complete bastards because you're obviously all complete nob-ends.

'Ah,' I hear you say, *'but I didn't buy it because I really want a guide on how to be a complete bastard, I bought it because it's obviously some sort of comedy book. I mean that's that bloke out of the Young Ones isn't it? And it could hardly be a serious book with a title like 'How To Be A Complete Bastard' now could it?'* Well that's where you're wrong matey boy, and if that's your attitude then why don't you just crap off!

Only joking! You see we're all bastards of one sort or another, and if you don't believe that there's a bit of the Bastard in you then why not try the litmus paper test — simply tear out this specially treated page, go to the toilet on it, and refer the resulting colour change to the chart below:

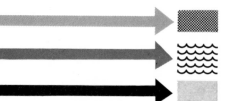

1 BROWN — I didn't mean that sort of going to the toilet. Shitty bastard.

2 YELLOW — Stupid dribbly bastard.

3 RED — Ha! Ha! Ha! Ha! Ha! Ha! Ha! Ha! Ha! Ha!

Let's face it you're in the right place for the litmus paper test aren't you? Because you're reading this book perched on the edge of the lavvy aren't you? Because you're either **a**) the mean bastard who hasn't bought a copy and who's avoiding one of those boring dinner parties downstairs by spending the whole time in the toilet where you just happen to have found this book, or **b**) the boring bastard who has those dinner parties and you think it's just so hip and groovy to keep books with slightly risqué titles in the toilet ('*No really, Torquil I don't see that the word 'Bastard' is at all offensive. After all, it really only means someone who was born out of wedlock*') because you think it'll impress your so-called friends. Well the joke's on you because for your information the title is on a peel off strip underneath which is printed 'How To Be A Complete C**t' — just try explaining that away to your parents if they happen to get to the toilet first! Even if you've got here first Mr Trendy Bastard, what are you going to do now? You've got a botty that's all streaky, the book in one hand, this soggy page in the other, and you can't reach the sink from the lavvy can you? Well you can, but it means waddling across the room with your pants round your ankles and you know how much that spreads the chocolate don't you? Well all I can say is *"Ha! Ha! Ha!",* thank you very much for your money, and I hope you have a crap life,

Adrian Edmondson.

Adrian Edmondson BA(stard)

7

How to read this book

1 Get someone to lock you into the lavvy from the outside with the equipment depicted in the picture below. Tell them not to let you out until they hear you laugh your bollocks off.

2 Plead for two hours with whoever locked you in to let you out because you've forgotten the book. Say,

"No, I'm serious, I really have forgotten the book."

Hammer on the door, plead, beg, grovel, threaten, make rash promises about agreeing to do your share of the cleaning, even round the back of the lavvy, threaten some more, until eventually the only method of escape dawns on you.

3 Cut off your bollocks and push them under the door.

4 Get the book and start again. (You may want to use the plaster at this point.)

5 Attempt to drink everything in sight, including the Domestos and Blue Stratos, but don't start reading until the pages look like they do in Fig 1.

BEFORE
Fig. 1

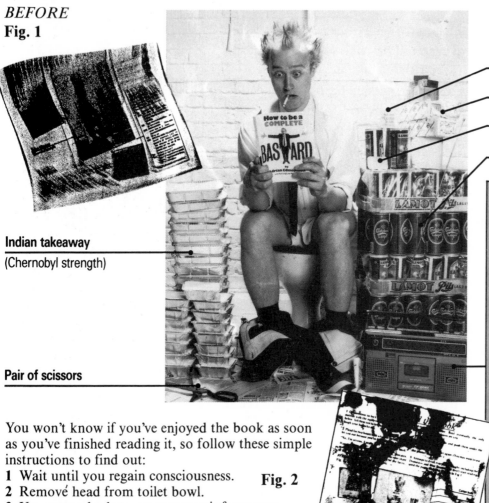

Indian takeaway

(Chernobyl strength)

Pair of scissors

Cotton buds

Fags

Plaster

Lager

THE TAPE-RECORDER
Useful for recording laughter, so that you can show all your friends how much you enjoyed the book. Here is a transcript of what happened when I read the book:

ME: Right here we go then.
SFX: 400 CANS OF LAGER BEING OPENED AND CONSUMED ALONG WITH 36 BIRYANIS AND 600 FAGS.
ME: Right, where's this book then … oh no, here it comes.
SFX: PAAAAAAAAAA ….. [Farty noise which lasts for 2½ hours] ….. AAAAAAARRRRRRPPPPPPP!!!!!!!
ME: Oh no, not …
SFX: RETCHING NOISE FOLLOWED BY WHAT SOUNDS LIKE 14 BUCKETS OF TAPIOCA HITTING THE GROUND AFTER BEING EMPTIED OFF THE TOP OF THE EMPIRE STATE BUILDING.
ME: Oh God, where am I?
SFX: SOUND OF FOOT SLIPPING ON A PIECE OF REGURGITATED ONION BHAJEE, THEN SOUND OF SKULL HITTING PORCELAIN.

"I hope you have as much fun as I did."

You won't know if you've enjoyed the book as soon as you've finished reading it, so follow these simple instructions to find out:
1 Wait until you regain consciousness.
2 Remové head from toilet bowl.
3 Use cotton buds to remove vomit from eyes.
4 If the pages look like they do in Fig 2, then you've enjoyed yourself.

Fig. 2

AFTER

GROWING UP
A
BASTARD

New Bastards start here ...

If you want to be a real bastard (as opposed to an unreal bastard like Jeffrey Archer), the kind of debonair "don't give a hang" toughie who thinks nothing of marketing Space Shuttle Jigsaw Puzzles or going into a Disabled toilet and loosening all the screws on the hand rails, then you really do have to start at the very beginning.

You see, being a total and utter and complete bastard is like learning to play the piano — except it's less girlie and boring and you don't have to wear frilly shirts or read music or have a totally nob-endie name like Liberace or Bobby Crush, and you don't get so fed up with being asked to play at parties that you eventually hack your hands off at the wrists — in fact it's not a bit like learning to play the piano at all really, so rip this bit out.

It's only like learning to play the piano because you've got to start young — but that's true of a lot of things, breathing, for one: so being a bastard is like breathing, then, or visiting the lavvy or going out with Britt Ekland.

If you're a member of the SPG you can skip the first 94 pages of this book. But the rest of you have got to go back to school ...

The Little Bastard's First Easy Reader

See Janet's ball

See John's chainsaw

Run, Spot, Run

Far too slow

Eeeeyowwwww, eeeeyowwww, eeeeyowwww

There are 54 new words in this book:

Agony	Exposed
Ambulance	Fart
Amputee	Hide
Anarchy	Horrible
And	In
Arm	Innards
Armalite	Janet
Artificial	Jism
respiration	John
Ball	Lacerate
Bits	Late
Bleed	Life support machine
Bogie	Limp
Bone	Mercy
Boner	No
Bonk-on	Parp!!
Brain death	Please open the
Bzzzzzzzzz	window
Chainsaw	Run
Chop	See
Clinically insane	Slaughter
Come	Slice
Cut	Stop!!!
Deep	The
Desperate	Too
Disembowel	Violence
Dog	Wicked
Eeeeyowwwww	Yelp

SCHOOL

HEADMASTER IN SHOCK OBSCENITIES SCANDAL

St Thomas's school was in the news again this week following the shock arrest of its long-serving headmaster, Mr William Gable.

Adrian Edmondson, aged nearly fourteen, and a pupil at the school, gave us details of the events leading up to the arrest.

It appears that Mr Gable was involved in a collision with a running (and, as yet, unidentified) pupil. Mr Gable was knocked to the ground and in the confusion which followed his briefcase apparently became open, spilling its contents all over the corridor. A number of pupils clearly saw copies of *Tuckshop*

Tease and *Beefy Prefect* amongst his official papers.

The police, who arrived within minutes, impounded the literature and took Mr Gable away.

Mr Gable, 54, and until very recently, married, denied all knowledge of the magazines and claimed that he was "set up b' some little bastard an' I've got a bloody goo' idea which one too, ar when I get my hands ' him his bottom will be sore he won't be able to down for a month."

He was then advised his lawyer to "Shut for Christ's sake".

THE QUEEN OF HEARTS
SHE MADE SOME TARTS
— IT WAS A RED-HOT
LESBO GANG-BANG.

SCRAPBOOK

Monsieur Farty→

THE FRENCH LETTER

Don't bother learning any French, just copy this out and send it to your stupid frog pen-pal (make sure it's a girlie, or you could be in for a big surprise):

LUCKY DIP! Girlies, I've got a REAL one pound note down my underpants!!! Why not jostle me at the bus stop at hometime. You could be a quid better off!!!
Adrian Edmondson *(the blond one in the blazer with the funny walk)*, 3P.

This is a picture of the recently completed Chemistry Laboratory Complex at St Thomas's school, after A. Edmondson of 3P "absolutely accidentally and by a complete fluke" managed to synthesize the exact formula for TNT.

Ma chère Simone,

Comment ca va ? Je suis très bien. C'est moi dans le photo sans touts les vêtements. C'est bon, n'est pas ? Très horny ?

Je tu veux venir a l'Angleterre pour les grandes vacances et pour encoulant dans la derriere. Je veux ouvrir ton jambes et tu manger jusqu'a mouris avec un sourir sur ta visage. J'espere tu aller comme un lapin parce-que j'encoule tres bien.

As-tu des grandes tits ? Je veux mettre ma tête les entres et aller, 'blub, blub, blub, blub.' Mon ami, Gavin, il demande s'il peut l'faire avec toi quand j'ennuie. J'ai le dit, 'Oui !!' J'ai vu son willy et il est presque comme grande si mon un. Tant pis !

J'espere que tu as bien. Ecris a moi bientôt et m'envoye votre panties.

Avec plusieurs des amour,
Ade X
Adrian Edmonson, 3P.

P.S. Donnes-tu tête ? Si non, tu ne visites pas moi o je te batterai très dur avec l'auto de mon pere.

13

PUNishment Book Extracts

DATE	NAME	REASON
12.2.74	Edmondson, A.	Immolation of school chemistry lab.
13.2.74	Edmondson, A.	Calling the French teacher "Monsieur Farty."
16.2.74	Edmondson, A.	Demonstrating his theory that 'the only thing first formers are good for is having their heads nailed to the desk with a railway spike.'
1.5.74	Edmondson, A.	Stealing punishment book.
3.5.74	Edmondson, A.	Making unlicensed firearms in T.D.
6.5.74	Edmondson, A.	Flashing at Miss Harris.
7.5.74	Riley, G.	Sending obscene polaroids to Miss Harris.
8.5.74	Edmondson, A.	Framing Riley, G.

A scene from the video we made during English lessons. I am saying "Go on Hamster, make my day."

14

A great shame this as I was building up quite an arsenal;

1. A fish that is a very cunningly disguised hand grenade (Pigs look for concealed weapons, never concealed fish.)

2. A ·44 Magnum disguised as a cricket bat.

3. A pipe-rack which actually folds into a knuckle duster.

Things to say in . . .

ENGLISH: "It's NOT bad grammar Sir, it's Joycean."

MUSIC: "Lemmy out of 'Motorhead' can't read music either Miss, but he earns a billion times more than you do, *and* gets off with loads of chicks, so what's the point?"

LATIN: "Excuse me Sir, but this is a comprehensive, and Latin isn't on the syllabus."

HISTORY: "James Joyce said, 'History is a nightmare from which I am trying to awake.' He was bloody spot on, wasn't he Sir?"

ART: "Miss, why did Andy Warhol get nude ladies to put their bosoms in tins of paint and then drag them across sheets of paper, and can you show us how it's done?"

The Secret Diary of ADRIAN 'THE COMPLETE BASTARD' EDMONDSON Aged 13¾

24th January
Got that crappy book about Adrian Mole for my birthday, and decided that if he can make a small fortune out of flogging a really boring diary about hardly anything at all, then the nitty gritty about my incredibly spicy life should bring in millions.

25th January
Skived off assembly and shagged Pandora behind the bike sheds instead. Smoked 40 N°6 during break. Lunch in the pub as usual, and as usual I got completely pissed. Ended up calling the headmaster a spotty turd and puking all over his car.

26th January
God these diaries are so bloody tedious to write. . . . . .

HOW TO BE THE BASTARD SCHOOL BULLY

1. Go round kicking people in the bollocks.

(That's about it really)

This is a cartoon I had published in the school magazine to reinforce respect for bullies:

"GIVE ME YOUR PACKET OF MONSTER MUNCH AND I'LL LET YOU LIVE"

"WAIT! MUMMY SAYS THAT ALL BULLIES ARE COWARDS AT HEART AND WILL RUN AWAY IF YOU STAND UP TO THEM"

"NO! YOU CAN'T HAVE MY PACKET OF MONSTER MUNCH, YOU NASTY BULLY!"

"MY MUMMY IS OBVIOUSLY A LYING BASTARD"

How To Be A BASTARD On BORING SCHOOL OUTINGS

Before you even get on the coach

- Ring the Pigs, give them the registration number, and report the coach as stolen.

On the coach

- *Hide 'Pee-Wee' Smith under the coats, fling open the rear emergency door and yell, "Sir, Sir!!! Pee-Wee Smith has fallen out of the emergency door and is currently bouncing his way down the fast lane of the motorway crying for his mummy."*

- *Throw Pee-Wee Smith out of the emergency door.*

- *Pass a note to the person in the seat in front of you saying, "By the time you have read this note I will have spewed up on your head."*

During the visit

- Spew on your worksheet so when the teacher collects them in you can say, "Sorry Sir, but I accidentally spewed all over my worksheet and my ballpoint won't write on vomit-coated paper, so I couldn't do it and had to spend my time in the cafeteria instead."

- If possible, disappear to the nearest pub. Always go with 'Strapper" Brantingham and not 'Pee-Wee' Smith, and never say anything pathetic like "Please Sir, can I have a cup of beer, please?" Say "Hi, bar guy. I'm just on my way to a fancy dress party for over 21's dressed as a schoolboy and I've just got time for you to lay a quick bevvie on me, OK?"

HOW TO BEHAVE LIKE A BASTARD IN A SCHOOL MEDICAL

School medicals are only OK if you like queueing in a freezing cold corridor with nothing on except your junior Y-fronts whilst everyone giggles at how skinny you are or the funny brown 'birthmark' that's rubbed off on the back of your pants, and going into the music room which is being used as a temporary clinic where an old man with hands the size of Pat Jennings pulls down your pants and holds your ball bag and says, '*cough*' whilst you try and look nonchalantly at the ceiling.

So why not ...

1 Show the boy in front of you a nudie book so that he gets a huge stiffie just before he goes in.

2 Make a pair of false testicles out of latex and two marbles. Put them down your pants and watch the doctor's face when they come away as you cough.

3 Urinate as soon as the doctor touches you.

THE COLLEGE BASTARD

College is totally and utterly a waste of time because not one of them does a really interesting course like "Chainsaw Studies", "How To Make Things Explode" or "The Life & Works of The Marquis de Sade".

And why not? Because all students are either utter arty spazmos who are always killing themselves because they can't come to terms with the fact that they're vegetarians, or anoraky science types with one inch wonkers and glasses so thick that light takes four minutes to get through and who think it's good to talk about 'quantum mechanics' at parties until you give into temptation and stuff their heads in the microwave until it goes 'ping'. And if you do go to college, you always end up lying in intensive care for two terms because of that homebrewed Deadly Nightshade wine some twat in Engineering III decided to bring to Jenny's party.

SO THE MOST IMPORTANT THING TO KNOW ABOUT ONCE YOU GET TO COLLEGE IS WHAT TO DRINK. AND THERE'S ONLY ONE DRINK THAT'S GUARANTEED TO GET YOU AS LEGLESS AS YOU WANT IN THE EVENING BUT STILL LEAVE YOU CONSCIOUS ENOUGH IN THE MORNING TO START POOHING NAPALM —

XX

MONSTER GET PISSED *FAST* LAGER

This will make you fall over!!!

The Lager Drinkers From Hell Wouldn't Give A

FUCKINGMONKEYBOLLOC

For Anything Else

THE BASTARD GUIDE TO FLAT SHARING

Ever since Homo Sapiens first shared his cave with others (and let's face it, it's not surprising with a name like that, is it matey boy?) One always stood out from the rest and become the leader, and in the "College Flat-sharing Environment" it's in your own interests to establish yourself in this position. Here's how:

1 Buy everyone else a can of "XXXXXXXXXX-XXXXXXXXX Monster Get Pissed Fast Lager".

2 Immediately suggest an election.

3 Take the voting slips to the "counting house".

4 Flush them down the lavvy and declare yourself outright winner. (Don't laugh, it's worked for Conservative Central Office twice already.)

5 Issue the following decree:

---

1 I hereby impose a levy of £1.47 per person to cover initial stationary and office requirements. (It is a coincidence that this is exactly the price of a can of "XXXXXXXXXXXXXXXXXXXX Monster Get Pissed Fast Lager.") [see Note 1]

2 It has been decided that the term "Collective living space organiser" is boring and smells of piss, and therefore the office shall be retitled:
"Generalissimo Supremo King of the Wild Frontier, Lordy Lordy his Majestyness, Doesn't he Look Great in Jodhpurs and a Greatcoat, Oh Great Big Grey Green Greasy Gracious One, Give him a Gun Somebody, he's so Get Down Funky and Sexy and Emperor of Everything and God and I bet he's got a Whopper, Master of the Lavvy, Master of the Scrolls (Ooer), Chief Lord High Priest and Whip Me if you Want to, Big Boy."

3 The word "democracy" shall be tippexed out of all books and replaced by "fatherly dictatorship", because let's face it, it's more like a family really, with one man taking responsibility for decisions which are more or less arrived at through consensus anyway. It's not some sort of tinpot totalitarian regime run by some megalomaniac authoritarian sadist who's going to ride roughshod over your personal liberties or show your stash of nudie mags to your parents when they visit. [see Note 2]

4 The following images must *not* be used for purposes of masturbation –
a) An 8–12–6 Great Western Locomotive
b) Bonnie Langford
c) Skippy the Bush Kangaroo
d) Me [see Note 1]

5 All girls brought to the flat must be positively vetted and undergo a total body search by me. Especially ones with big Wally Jumblatts.

Note 1: Except me.
Note 2: Offenders to be shown their own nudie mags then have their personal liberties and engorged squiggy bits ridden roughshod over with a lawnmower.

*It's simply a question of knowing
which societies to join:*

*Nothing wrong
with this society
— a must for all
bastards!*

The Fresher's Handbook

RUGBY CLUB

Come and join us!
1 Lots of drinking.
2 Shoving tampons up each other's bums.
3 More drinking.
4 Sing 'Here We Go' all the way to Carlisle, forget to get off the coach, and sing 'I'm A Stupid Dicky-Di-Do Bastard And The Hairs On My Zulu Warrior Hang Down To My Eskimo Nell' all the way back.
5 Drink your own piss!!!
6 Do fantastic impressions with your genitals:
   ● Meat 'n' two veg
   ● Barry Manilow
   ● Bucks Fizz
7 Annual 'Mile of Ale' Competition.
8 Shit your own pants for a dare.
9 Sometimes we play rugby!

FEMINIST SOC.

If you're interested in contemporary feminist issues and wish to get involved, please join us.

*JOIN THIS SOC!! All
the members are girls!
All-night stormy sex
sessions guaranteed!
(Remember — they're
desperate)*

MOUNTAINEERING SOC.

Salutations! Thanks to increased funding last term, we have purchased the following new equipment:
1 piton, 1 ice axe, 140 armbands, 15 banners, 30 cap badges, and 1 replica luger, so now is the best time ever for "right-thinking" people to join in this, the dawn of our glorious ascension.
   Experienced mountaineers positively discouraged.

*The only interesting thing
about mountaineering is
that the word crampon
sounds a bit like tampon!*

TEDDY BEAR SOC.

A teddy is a fresher's best friend! Join us with yours for picnics, singsongs, talks by Michael Bond etc. Getting through your first term will be un-bear-able without us! No Care Bears.

*Obviously the Neo-Nazi
Soc. Join at once in
full regalia.*

EXTREMELY DANGEROUS SPORTS SOC.

Always looking for new members.

GIRLS! GIRLS! GIRLS!

Wanted for non-sexist, but extremely
arty radical 35mm film, provisionally
entitled *Sin Slaves in Leather*.

See A. Edmondson, Film Soc.

EXIT

Confidential advice for mature students, students with exam
pressures or low marks in mocks, and those with relationship
problems. Bring your own plastic bag and hairy string.

INTERNATIONAL MARXISTS

Join the class struggle! Make your voice heard! Power to the
Proletariat! (Please note: we are tired of smart-arsed gits coming
along, dressed as Groucho, Chico, Harpo or Zeppo and saying
pratty things like, "As Marx once said, 'I shot an elephant in my
pyjamas yesterday...'")

If you are one of these people, join the Marxist-Leninists
instead; then you can go, "As Lenin once said, 'I am the walrus,
goo goo ga joob.'" Ha bloody ha.

PAN-ISLAMIC SOC.

آأبـبثـبثبثبثـج خـجخجذذذزززشـشـشـشـش ضـضـض
ننةهههةووللالايي REAGAN مـمـمغغغفـفـفة

FREE NELSON MANDELA SOC.

We think the name of the society explains it all, OK?

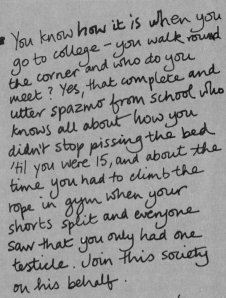

(Handwritten marginal notes:)

You know how it is when you go to college – you walk round the corner and who do you meet? Yes, that complete and utter spazmo from school who knows all about how you didn't stop pissing the bed 'til you were 15, and about the time you had to climb the rope in gym when your shorts split and everyone saw that you only had one testicle. Join This society on his behalf.

Join as a helper! Don't ask for advice, don't accept anything to eat there (especially Smarties) and don't turn your back on them to admire the view from the window.

Join, get pally with the chairman, take him to the union bar, get him totally pissed and suggest a game of 'Simon Says'. Start off with a few routine ones then go, "Simon says, Yell really loudly, like at the top of your voice until your lungs bleed, 'Ronald Reagan is a really good bloke...'"

A great society! Obviously either totally pissed when they wrote this, or full of nubile girlie secs learning Pitmans.

Join at once and claim your free Nelson Mandela.

HOW TO BE A SEXIST BASTARD

"HOW TO BE A SEXY BASTARD MORE LIKE!"

All women love a bastard. It's the best known fact in the whole world that girlies like to be dominated and stepped all over — well, all of them except the stupid Feminist types but you can soon spot them by the predictable Feministy things they say:

Typical feministy sayings:

* "No" (the biggest Feministy giveaway of all).
* "Go away and leave me alone."
* "No, I don't want to sleep with you. Never, ever."
* "No, I don't come here often."
* "No, I don't want to dance."
* "I'm already going out with someone." (Probably another Feminist!)
* "I can't; I'm washing my hair Friday."
* "Look, just fuck off and leave me alone."
* "Get your hands out of my bra, whoever you are."
* "Not even for a million pounds ..."
* "Go away, or my boyfriend will hit you."
* "No I'm sorry, I'm washing my hair every night for the rest of my life."
* "That's it, I'm calling the police."

"I'M SO BLOODY SEXY!"

   WARNING: Some Feminists pretend not to be Feminists and agree to go home with you, but as soon as you drop your pants they collapse in paroxysms of laughter and say:
   "What's that?"
   or "Where is it?"
   or "Have you had a sex change or what?"

In my experience 99.999999999% of girlies are Feminists, which means you're pretty likely to come across one sooner or later. When you do, and she refuses to lie down and let you do squiggy things with her, like she's supposed to, and starts giving you all that Womens' Lib crap instead, here's how to put her in her place and make her feel two inches tall ("which is just about the size of your nob" as a Feminist would say):

Feministy Propaganda	The Bastard's Response
Women can do anything a man can do	Oh yeah? Well how many girlies can get a huge great stonk-on then? Or keep goal as well as Peter Shilton? Or win the men's 400 metres? Or even do a wee standing up without getting their feet wet, like at least 40% of us men? (Check your shoes before saying this.)
Women are entitled to a career	I fully agree. They're very good at being pin-ups, blue movie actresses, prostitutes and tea ladies, and they shouldn't be discouraged.
Women should have equal pay	Why? They always get the bloke to pay for everything, and anyway, they'd only waste it all on crap like lip gloss, eye liner, contraceptives, Mills & Boon novels, big posters of Richard (bumface) Gere and Tampax. They should only get more money if they agree to spend it on saucy underwear, silicon implants, Lager, or me.
Housewives should receive a wage for their duties	Why? How long does it take to clean a house? Ten minutes? I wouldn't mind that job — sitting on my bum all day in my dressing-gown, painting my toe-nails, watching Australian soap operas, scoffing boxes of chocolates and having it off with the milkman. (I might skip the last one, though.)
Women are always portrayed as sex objects	And not surprisingly! Who'd want to see a pair of bollocks on page 3? Who'd stick them all over the factory wall, or call their mates over and say, "Cor! Look at these bollocks!" Or, "Blimey! I wish my missus had bollocks like that!"

"LOOK OUT, HERE COMES SEXPANTS EDMONDSON!"

SURE-FIRE PICK-UP LINES
for the
Smoochy
BASTARD

1 "What's a beautiful girl like you doing sitting on the end of my nob? Oops, sorry — wishful thinking."

2 "Look here's the deal: I buy you a Babycham and you surrender your body to me for the night — now what could be fairer than that?"

3 "That's a really bad set of teeth you've got. Let me get you pregnant and you'll get free dental treatment."

4 "Go on. I'll give you a fiver."

5 "You're really ugly and I'll be doing you a favour."

6 "Alright, make it a tenner, but you'd better wriggle a lot."

7 "If I said you had a beautiful body, would you swallow ten inches?"

8 "They call me the 'roadie' because I'm the one carrying the heavy equipment." (Be careful not to say: ". . . because I'm the one carrying all the amplifiers and speakers from the van into the hall where the band are going to do the gig.")

9 "Behold and rejoice, for you are the most favoured over all women. I am the Angel Gabriel and I have been sent by the Lord God Almighty to do some really serious bonking with you."

10 "Go on, please, I'm desperate. I haven't had a shag in ten years — I mean I'm a virgin, well, technically speaking. In fact I'm a homosexual, but I think you could convert me because you look like a man: sort of a halfway house really . . ."

If the "sure-fire" pick-up lines don't work, one totally brilliant way to get tons of girlies is to set up your own dating agency. Then you actually get them to PAY for the privilege of doing incredibly saucy things to you.

Come and get it while it's hot!! Because it's ACTION, ACTION, ACTION all the way once you're on DREAM DATE's books. We have the man of your dreams on our Digiton 2000 Stud-Finder Computer just waiting for you to drag him off and give him a good seeing-to. The perfect man, guaranteed no little fat acne-ridden train-spotting emotionally crippled social nobodies on our books, matey boy, just pure hunks of beef with IQs, wallets and posing pouches to match!

No matter who you're looking for, we've got him. Honest.

• *DOES DREAM DATE REALLY WORK?*
You bet your hymens it does!! Just listen to what three of our clients have to say:

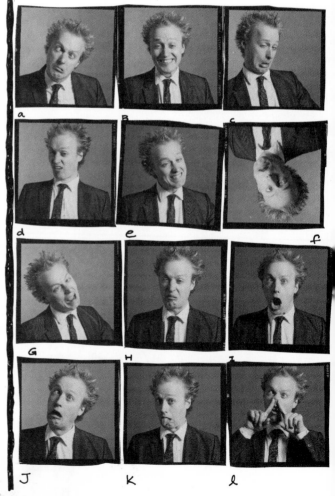

UNATTACHED?   LONELY?   DESPERATE?
– *join the club…*

The Adrian Edmondson

Dream Date
Bureau

Mandy & Sheik Abdulla Edmondson

Mandy never thought in a million, billion years that she'd meet, and fall in love with, a real Arabian prince. "Sheik Abdulla Edmondson totally swept me off my feet! Ever since that first date when we broke the bank at 'La Wimpy' casino in Monte Carlo, life has been one long orgy of careless spending. The Prince is a real gentleman and an absolutely brilliant bloke. The best thing I've ever done in the whole world was to apply to DREAM DATE."

Lindsey & Adrian "Chuck" Norris

"'Chuck' is everything I've ever looked for in a man. I practically shat myself when DREAM DATE fixed me up with the World's Number One martial artist and international movie star! I've been so busy going to endless Hollywood parties that I haven't even had time to do all the usual girlie things like paint my nails, read soppy books and talk crap. I've met tons of famous producers and directors and I'm going to be in my own movie soon! DREAM DATE, you're a star yourself!"

Tracey & King Adriano of Latvia

"Being incredibly buxom but working class, I thought a painter & decorator was all I'd get, but DREAM DATE made me realise I was talking out of my arsehole. They fixed me up with none other than King Adriano of Latvia. What a hunk! I couldn't stop myself slobbering all through dinner with this bloke, and I didn't even mind paying for it when he said, 'Oh dear, I seem to have left my chest of jewels on the bus.' Cheers, DREAM DATE! You should charge ten times as much."

Would you consider yourself:
- ☐ Outgoing
- ☐ Confident
- ☐ Adventurous
- ☐ Dominant
- ☐ Gullible
- ☐ Squeamish about surprises, especially ones involving an industrial-sized tin of Swarfega, two rabbit-shaped jelly moulds and a welsh corgi called Roy.

Do your interests include:
- ☐ Theatre
- ☐ Cinema
- ☐ Horseriding
- ☐ Photography
- ☐ Conversation
- ☐ Politics
- ☐ Sports
- ☐ Walking
- ☐ Sailing
- ☐ 4 hours of pre-marital sex and no questions asked

Which of the men opposite comes the closest to your perfect **DREAM DATE?**

FIVE MINUTE PERSONALITY PROFILE:
Are you, by any chance, the heiress to an incredibly vast fortune which you will be inheriting very, very soon?
☐ Yes   ☐ No

Do you have any jealous ex-boyfriends lurking in the background like, say, Royal Marines or truck drivers, who might want to break your DREAM DATE's legs?
☐ Yes   ☐ No

Would you be annoyed if a man said he had a really enormous willy but it wasn't, well, quite so huge, when it came down to it?
☐ Yes   ☐ No

Would you want your money back in the unlikely event that your DREAM DATE didn't live up to all your expectations?
☐ Yes   ☐ No

Do you know Kung Fu or any of that stuff?
☐ Yes   ☐ No

OK DREAM DATE, YOU'VE UTTERLY AND TOTALLY CONVINCED ME AND I'M IN YOUR HANDS. I ENCLOSE £25 AND A NUDE PHOTO OF MYSELF.

PLEASE RUSH ME MY DREAM DATE RIGHT NOW!!
I'M HOT AND READY!

Name . . . .

Address . . . .

. . . .

Nearest bus service to place of residence . . . .

Send to: The Adrian Edmondson DREAM DATE Bureau
PO Box 23, London W1.

A BASTARD GUIDE TO
CONTRACEPTION

(OR HOW TO ROUND OFF A ROMANTIC EVENING BY GETTING YOUR GIRLIE PREGNANT FOR A LAU

If she's on the pill, there's not much you can do, but if she uses a diaphragm you might just be able to switch it for the carburettor gasket out of a Ford Fiesta XR2 with sun-roof and alloy wheels. However, if it's down to the good old johnny, you suddenly have a lot more scope...

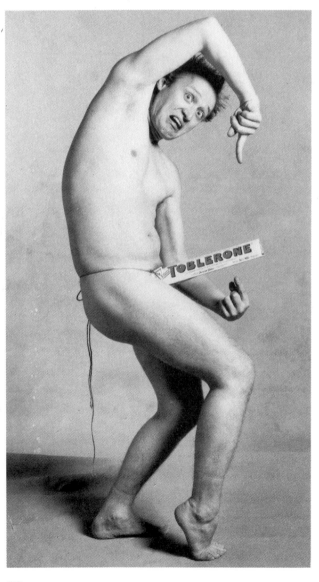

TRYING TO GET AWAY WITH NOT WEARING ONE

- "You're so ugly I probably won't come anyway"
- "It's OK, I used to work at Sellafield"
- "I've had a mastectomy"
- "Let's use the rhythm method" (any record by Stockhausen or Bananarama will do)
- "These 'Spartan Invisibles' sure are extra-sensitive aren't they?"

BUT IF SHE INSISTS ...

... here's some

a shuttlecock

a sock

a Tesco's bag and hairy string

a fish

an Action Man deep-sea diver's helmet

a jam doughnut

THINGS GUARANTEED TO KILL ANY *"Special Moment"* STONE DEAD

After one night you're probably pretty bored and cheesed off, and rarin' to tangle with the next steaming sex kitten in the queue.

However, if, as usual, you were just too bloody totally and utterly good in bed again, and Miss "Has Been" is hooked on your moves like . . . er . . . well . . . like a fish that's been caught by someone using a rod, and a line, with a sort of hook on the end of it, here are some ways to convey the message that she's not welcome around your parts anymore:

- Get out a felt-tipped pen and draw a line straight down her face.
- Tell her you've got two tickets for the Paul Daniels Magic Show.
- Play charades and mime "Fuck Off!"
- Say, "In this light you look just like Jon Pertwee."
- Say, "I was once a woman, you know."
- Ask her if she was once a man.
- Show her what you just found up your nose.
- When you're in the cinema together suddenly scream out: "STOP CRYING! I AM NOT GOING TO GIVE YOU ANOTHER PORTION. I WANT TO WATCH THE KIA-ORA COMMERCIAL WITH MY HEAD THE RIGHT WAY UP!!!"
- In the restaurant, shout out "This tartar sauce tastes just like my spunk, doesn't it?"

COMPLETELY unsafe contraceptives to use:

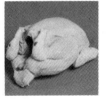

an oven-ready chicken   *a rubber glove*   *an ice cream cone (eat the ice cream first)*   *a piece of fruit*   *any vacuum cleaner attachment*   *Leon Brittan*

THE BASTARD IN BED

1

ME: HANG ON, I'D BETTER TURN THE LIGHTS OUT BECAUSE YOU'RE SO UGLY I'LL PROBABLY BE SICK IF I CAN SEE YOUR FACE.

2

3

RIGHT...
YOU READY ?...
BRACE YOURSELF...
HERE I COME.

GIRLIE: IS THAT IT ?

ME: OH GOD! TALK! TALK! TALK! THAT'S ALL YOU WOMEN EVER DO! LOOK — YOU'VE HAD YOUR FUN, NOW EITHER GET UP AND LEAVE OR SHUT UP AND GO TO SLEEP.

6

7

GIRLIE: WELL AT LEAST LET ME HAVE THE HOT WATER BOTTLE.

ME: THAT'S NOT THE HOT WATER BOTTLE, THAT'S MY COLOSTOMY BAG. THAT BIRYANI'S REALLY MADE IT SIZZLE.

9

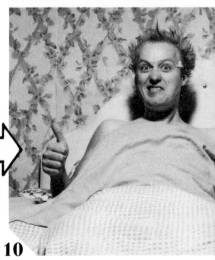

10

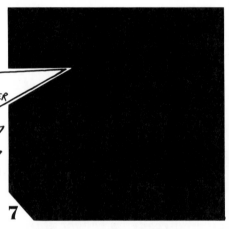

4

ME: RIGHT, WHERE'S THE STOPWATCH?
HEY! ONLY 3 SECONDS FROM START
TO FINISH. IMPRESSIVE OR WHAT?!

5

ME: NIGHT THEN.

GIRLIE: SOB! BOO HOO!

ME: AND STOP
CRYING !!!

8

GIRLIE: I'M FEELING SAD,
I NEED A CUDDLE.

ME: WELL I'M FEELING
KNACKERED AFTER THAT
SEX MARATHON AND I
NEED SOME SLEEP, SO
SHUT THE FUCK UP!

AAAHHH!!!

31

HOW TO EXPOSE YOURSELF WITHOUT GETTING ━━ARRESTED

1 **HAVE YOUR NOB MAKE HISTORY SO THAT IT HAS TO BE SHOWN ON THE TV NEWS:**

a Get your nob to take over from Kojak for a week.

b Get your nob to raise the Titanic.

c Lay it down over a puddle for Fergie to walk over.

2 **GET YOUR NOB ON "THAT'S LIFE":**

a Write to Esther and say your girlfriend thinks you have a nob that looks like a potato.

b Complain that you bought some 'Erecto-Stiffie Guaranteed-Twelve-Inches-Of-Lead Stud-O-Cream' and it didn't work. Send photos in as evidence and then insist Esther takes your nob out into the streets to test it.

c Teach your nob to say "sausages."

Note: *A lot of people think my nob's on "That's Life" all the time, but that isn't my nob, that's Esther Rantzen.*

Totally BASTARD Things To Do
Number 1

Join the *Samaritans*

———————————— *R I N G R I N G !... R I N G R I N G !...*

ME: Hello, Samaritans.

CALLER: Look it's no good, I just can't cope anymore. My own parents have kicked me out of the family home because I'm "just too bloody completely horrible, boring and spotty, and why didn't we have a gerbil instead of you, then at least we could have had it put down without a police inquiry"; and my girlfriend's left me because, as she put it, "she didn't know she was going out with me in the first place and didn't know that some jerk waving to her across a crowded pub three years ago was a sign that we were engaged"; and to top it all I think I'm going to remain a virgin all my life because my nob's too small. There's nothing left for me in this world so I think I'm going to kill myself.

ME: Oh, that's interesting. How are you going to do it?

CALLER: I'm going to hang myself.

ME: Well, make sure you've got the right kind of rope.

CALLER: Pardon?

ME: I said make sure you've got the right sort of rope. If you get that stretchy rope you'll find that when you jump it stretches, so instead of breaking your neck instantaneously it just suffocates you slowly until your tongue bursts and your eyes pop out like champagne corks. And if it's really stretchy you might find you jump off your chair or whatever and just bounce up and down hitting the floor occasionally, and since you've tied your hands behind your back you can't get yourself free, and you'll probably end up vomiting yourself to death.

CALLER: Hang on a minute ... I thought you were supposed to talk me out of killing myself.

ME: Why? I thought you said you couldn't take it anymore and that topping yourself was the only way out?

CALLER: Yes but ... look, this is the Samaritans isn't it?

ME: What? No, this is the "Really Sexy Escort Agency Ltd."

CALLER: Oh sorry, I thought this was the number for the Samaritans.

ME: No, you must have the wrong number, this is the "Really Sexy Escort Agency Ltd.", incorporating "Girls Who Do Just About Whatever You Want Them To Do For Hardly Any Money At All, Co. & Sons Ltd.".

CALLER: Oh ... how much is "Hardly Any Money At All"?

ME: Oh ... about 5p.

CALLER: 5p ! ! ! ! !

ME: Oh alright then, to you, 4p.

CALLER: 4p ! ! ! ! !

ME: Blimey you drive a hard bargain, alright then, 2p, but I can't go any lower. Now what would you like?

CALLER: Well what have you got?

ME: Absolutely everything, just describe your fantasy and we shall provide it for you.

CALLER: Well, in that case I'll have ... an Anita Harris lookalike ... smeared with pineapple and banana yoghurt ... wrapped in clingfilm ... with ...

ME: Ha! Ha! Ha! Ha! Haaa! Had you! April Fool!! Of course this is the Samaritans! Now, what seems to be the problem? (PAUSE)   Hello? Hello?

(SOUND OF CHAIR SCRAPING ALONG THE FLOOR, THEN THE SOUND OF SOMEONE BOUNCING UP AND DOWN AND HITTING THE FLOOR OCCASIONALLY)

Ring the Samaritans YOURSELF

RING RING!... RING RING!...

SAMARITAN: Hello, Samaritans, how may we help you?

░░░░BLAM! *(SOUND OF GUNSHOT)*

ME: Bloody Hell! Missed!!!

SAMARITAN: Hello, hello, are you alright?

ME: No of course I'm not alright.

SAMARITAN: What seems to be the problem?

ME: Well I don't seem to be able to get this pump-action twelve-bore shotgun into my mouth *and* pull the trigger at the same time.

SAMARITAN: But why would you want to do that!?

ME: Well how else am I going to shoot my bloody brains out?

SAMARITAN: Look don't do anything rash! Nothing is that serious! A problem shared is a problem halved! Talk to me, I'm your friend!

ME: Look there's only one way you're going to stop me from killing myself, and that's if you say something for me.

SAMARITAN: What's that? Anything! I'll say anything!

ME: I want you to say "The only way to kill yourself with a shotgun is to tie a piece of string round the trigger, wrap it round something, and then pull it."

SAMARITAN: What? Oh alright! The only way to kill yourself with a shotgun is to tie a piece of string round the trigger, wrap it round something, and then pull it.

ME: Is it? Oh, thank you very much.

FIRE THE GUN THEN THROW A LARGE TRIFLE AGAINST THE FRIDGE DOOR, AND LISTEN TO THE RESULTANT FARTY BLUBBERY MESS ON THE OTHER END OF THE TELEPHONE.

The Statue of
BASTARDY

1 Try an "Eddie Kidd"-type "Leap of Death" over 40 nuns.
See if you can beat the record of ½ a nun.

How to be a COMPLETE BASTARD TO THE DEAF

Go like this:

Or if you want to save some time, go like this:

How To Be A BASTARD

in the SHOE SHOP

1

ME: *I'd like a pair of DMs please, Mr Assistant. Size 10.*
ASSISTANT: *Certainly sir.*

On A Steamroller

2	Try it again.
3	Try it again.
4	Run over the man from the *Guinness Book of Records*.

2

ME: *Can I try them out?*
ASSISTANT: *Certainly sir.*

3

ASSISTANT: *Ooooofffffff!*

4

ME: *I'll take them!*

People say that your personality changes for the worse when you get behind the wheel. Well this is absolutely brilliant, because if you're already a bit of a bastard to begin with, you'll be an even bigger and utterly total bastard when you get in your car.

How To Transform Your FORD SIERRA Into A TOTAL DEATH MACHINE

1. Have it regularly serviced by a Ford dealer.
2. Modify it yourself.

— WHO'S CAR? ROAD TEST —

The Ford Sierra
BASTARDMOBILE

PERFORMANCE ☆☆☆☆☆

The secret of its speed lies in the minor modifications Mr Edmondson has made under the bonnet. Out went the standard 1600 OHV engine in favour of a Rolls-Royce V12 Merlin aero engine — from what was, until recently, the last flying Spitfire in England.

An interesting feature we discovered quite by accident was the car's ability to reach its top speed in reverse (which is where we expected third gear to be.)

Mr Edmondson showing off the Bastardmobile's "bloody big engine."

HANDLING & RIDE ☆ ☆ ☆

The first thing you notice is that the car turns the opposite way to the direction of the steering wheel. This system was designed by Mr Edmondson as an anti-theft device. Unfortunately, he "absolutely and completely forgot" to inform us of its presence, but once we'd agreed to pay for the damage to his front garden, we set out on our test route: a mixture of town, country lane and motorway driving.

First impressions were of excessive understeer, uncontrolled torque fightback out of fast bends and badly weighted steering. Mr Edmondson told us the reason for this was that he'd had to throw a lot of bits out to make room for his "lager stash."

REFINEMENT ☆ ☆

Refinement is quite good, although engine noise becomes irritable after a short while ("Silencers are for virgins who have testicles the size of sultanas," explained Mr Edmondson.)

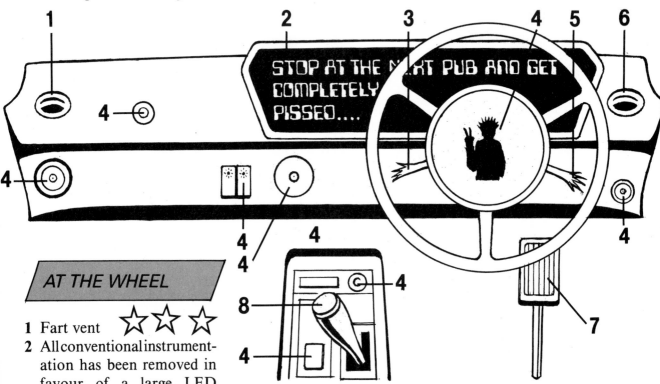

AT THE WHEEL ☆ ☆ ☆

1 Fart vent
2 All conventional instrumentation has been removed in favour of a large LED display panel which flashes up messages like "Drive faster Mr Hardly-Any-Nob-At-All", and "Overtake!! Overtake!! Tora! Tora! Tora!"
3 The broken stem of the indicators ("I prefer to indicate with my fingers.")
4 Horn
5 The broken stem of the light switch makes use of lights impossible ("To avoid confusion with safety-conscious Volvos and Saabs.")
6 Air vent
7 Just one pedal which performs all three functions of Brake, Clutch and Accelerator. (Mr Edmondson believes that the "Pot Luck" factor relieves the boredom of motorway driving.)
8 Joke gear lever

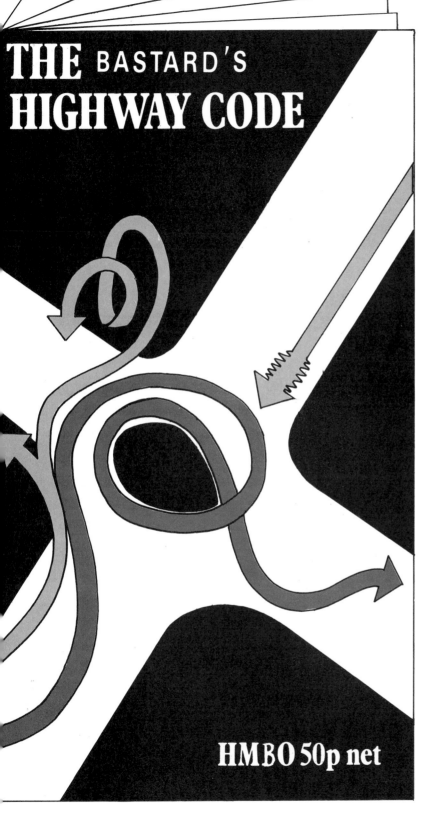

THE BASTARD'S HIGHWAY CODE

HMBO 50p net

Signals by persons with a big blue tit on their head

"Hello mate!"

"Corr!! Look at the bristols on her over there!"

"I'm just going for a quick one off the wrist"

NO HAND SIGNALS – *DRIVER WANKING*

Signals to other road users

"I am going to turn the car over"

"I've just dropped a big one"

"Bloody Hell! Half my car's gone missing"

"Oh no, there it is"

"I am sitting in the back seat and this car is completely out of control"

"I am completely pissed"

"I'm more pissed than I thought I was"

"I am driving with my nob"

"Oh God! It's gone again and now I'm just trying to keep my balance"

"I have got no brakes"

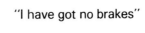

Pedestrians – *be seen at night*

Overtaking
REMEMBER:

MIRROR ....SIGNAL ....RAM THE BASTARD OFF THE ROAD

HOW TO HOLD YOUR OWN
KAMIKAZE
DEATH
SQUADRON
RALLY:

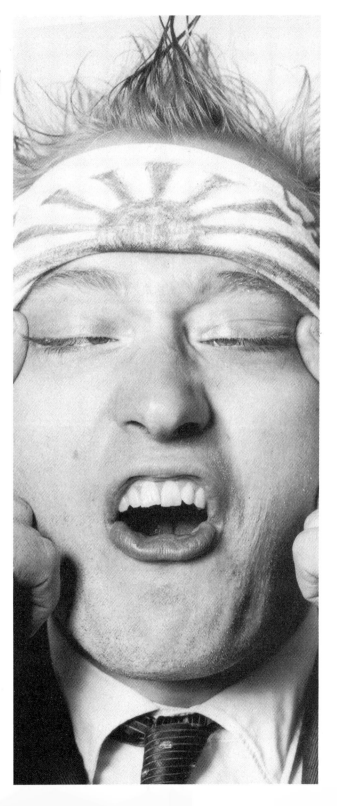

All you need for my Kamikaze Death Squadron Rally are:

- 2 or more competitors & vehicles
- 1 copy of the Highway Code
- 1 blowtorch

HOW TO PLAY:

a First burn your copy of the Highway Code. You won't be needing it.

b Competitors may use any route they wish providing that they follow the two main rules:

RULE 1 — All road signs/signals must be treated as if they gave exactly the OPPOSITE order.

i.e. Red traffic light = Go
'No right turn' = Turn right ahead
'No entry' = Entry permitted
'Give way' = Keep on going as fast as you can.

RULE 2 — You must always drive at double the speed limit.

i.e. 30 mph becomes 60mph (If wet, treble the speed limit. i.e. 70mph becomes 210mph.)

THE WINNER:

Is the person who reaches the destination first, or in the case of no vehicles whatsoever finishing and being written off within ½ miles of the start, the competitor with the least severe head injuries.

HOW TO CUT THROUGH RED TAPE

1 **Get chainsaw**
2 **Get red tape**
3 **Cut through red tape with chainsaw**

(Well what do you expect for £3.95 you stupid bastards?)

Club
BASTARD

'GUARANTEED SHAGGING'

'ROUND THE CLOCK DRINKING'

'INCREDIBLE AMOUNTS OF
GIRLS WITH BIG TITS'

'MINDLESS VIOLENCE'

TITLE	
INITIALS	
SURNAME	
NICKNAMES	
ROOM TYPE	
BLOOD TYPE	

*I wish to pay the £154 supplement
for my own dialysis machine* ☐

CONDITIONS

1 No money will be refunded if there are no women whatsoever on this trip.
2 If, in the unlikely event we alter your departure airport, day of departure, hotel, apartment or resort where you have booked, and you end up in a tent at the end of Luton Airport runway, we'll piss ourselves laughing for days.
3 The price of your holiday will be the brochure price plus anything else we add on.

INDEMNITY

I'm a big boy and I know what I'm doing and if I get banged up in some Dago jail on a trumped-up charge for 25 years, that's my doing, and I won't seek a penny compensation from my mates at **CLUB BASTARD**.

Signature ....

Date ....

Club BASTARD
BOOKING FORM

NEXT OF KIN DETAILS

NAME ....
ADDRESS ....
....
HOME NO ....
WORK NO ....

HAVE YOU MADE A WILL?

☐ YES   ☐ NO

Getting There

10.00 Meet in the Duty Free lounge at Gatwick; start drinking.
11.00 Board chartered 737 to Malaga.
11.05 Inflate lifejackets in mid-flight.
11.20 Mile High Club (This may not be available on some flights).
11.55 Impromptu visit to flight deck; five-minute flying lesson. Scare Dago radar.

Your Itinerary for Day One

12.15 Arrive at Malaga Airport; welcome scuffle with Spanish police armed with deportation orders, CS Gas and Water Cannons.
14.00 Wreck hotel.
14.30 'Drink Yourself Unconscious' competition.

CLUB BASTARD

'You're only stupid once!'

Imagine the scene: sitting under a shady palm listening to the chirrupping of the cicadas as the sun sets majestically in the west; Sipping at an exotic cocktail as you watch the little fishing boats cruise into the bustling whitewashed harbour. And the knowledge that all you have to do is go up to any woman you want and say *'I'm from Club Bastard and I claim my free bird'* and she'll sit on your face.

'If you're a virgin then this is the place for you!'

THE RESORT - *TOSSA*

Tossa has lots of restaurants, bars, discos and cafes where the waiters speak such abysmal English you're sure to be able to start an argument or a bottle fight at the slightest provocation, keeping you busy every second of your stay. If you're finding it difficult to start a fight don't worry - your **Club Bastard** Rep will organise a 'Keep Gibraltar British' day, with a march and sing-song through the town.

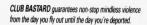

CLUB BASTARD guarantees non-stop mindless violence from the day you fly out until the day you're deported.

Hotel Turdos

The Turdos has become a firm Club Bastard favourite over the past few years, and has been completely rebuilt for the start of the season. It is famed for its delicate Byzantine architecture including a huge, beautiful stained-glass window above the lobby entrance, and intricate marble and onyx pillars which support the dining-room roof (rebuilt in 1976, 1977 (twice), 1978, 1979, 1980, 1982, 1983, 1984 and 1985). An air-conditioned bar is constantly kept full of the strongest local spirits and beers, so there's no excuse for not rampaging and vomiting violently through the corridors each night, and trying to stuff fire extinguishers up your bum.

YOUR **CLUB BASTARD** REP

The **Club Bastard** reps are the life and soul of the party, and are selected with one main thing in mind - they really have to like Paul Daniels. They can out-drink, out-sweat, out-puke, out-fall-over-unconscious, and out-end-up-in-a-Spanish-jail absolutely everyone. They're absolutely bloody great, and they're always completely pissed (which seems to turn on the ladies).

Look out for these symbols which tell you what's on and where:

Abusing foreigners

Organised punch-ups with Club Kraut Bastard

Spanish Tummy

Page 3 girls

Organised Farting Contests

Great Gobbing off the Balcony Contests

Birdy Song

BASTARD *Ways To Make* LOTS OF MONEY

1. Own A Brothel

This sounds like a dream, like owning your own pub, but I haven't figured out how to do it yet. I mean, it's hard enough to get even one girlie at the best of times, let alone enough to run a business. You can't advertise for "Saucy flibbertygibbets" in the Evening Standard and Alfred Marks say they only deal in secretarial recruitment (which I thought was the same thing).

Would someone please tell me how it's done?

2 Run A Protection Racket in Covent Garden

This is a dead easy way to make piles of cash. You simply go round to all the restaurants, wine bars and overpriced porcelain knick-knack shops in Covent Garden and say that if they don't pay you vast sums of money, you'll do a satirical mime about them.

3. Become A Lawyer

4. Extortion

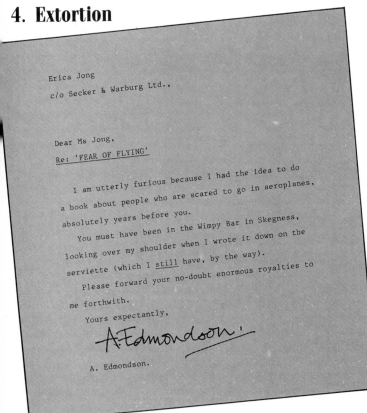

```
Erica Jong
c/o Secker & Warburg Ltd.,


Dear Ms Jong,
Re: 'FEAR OF FLYING'

    I am utterly furious because I had the idea to do
a book about people who are scared to go in aeroplanes,
absolutely years before you.
    You must have been in the Wimpy Bar in Skegness,
looking over my shoulder when I wrote it down on the
serviette (which I still have, by the way).
    Please forward your no-doubt enormous royalties to
me forthwith.
    Yours expectantly,

    A. Edmondson!

    A. Edmondson.
```

Try writing to rich authors, saying they've ripped off your idea, and demanding compensation:

5. Theft

Knock on someone's door wearing a radiation suit. Say:
"I am the Four Minute Warning — they couldn't put it out on the telly because of the snooker."
As soon as they have buried themselves under several mattresses and the kitchen door, you can wander round the house stealing their knick-knacks – and I don't mean their underwear (well whatever turns you on really).

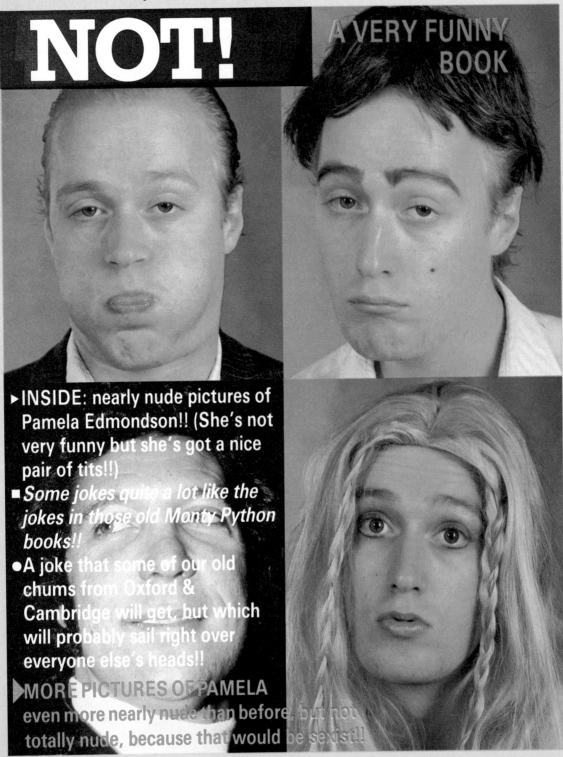

Write a book that really isn't very funny and rip off the kids.

NOT!

A VERY FUNNY BOOK

▶ INSIDE: nearly nude pictures of Pamela Edmondson!! (She's not very funny but she's got a nice pair of tits!!)

■ *Some jokes quite a lot like the jokes in those old Monty Python books!!*

● A joke that some of our old chums from Oxford & Cambridge will get, but which will probably sail right over everyone else's heads!!

▶ MORE PICTURES OF PAMELA even more nearly nude than before, but not totally nude, because that would be sexist!!

Rip Off Poor Pathetic Pervies

Simply publish a magazine that promises really spicy nudie action so that the pervies buy it in droves. Like this:

FULL-COLOUR
PUSSY
The Monthly Magazine For Pussy Lovers Everywhere

Price:
£1.20

★ **READERS' PHOTOS EXTRAVAGANZA!**

● **Dr Jenny's Clinic!**

▶ **KITTY & FLUFF GET IT ON!**

● **Penny** *– au naturale!*

■ **PUSS IN BOOTS!**

PUSSY EATING!

● ***Tom & Jemimah, TOGETHER!***

★ ***Cream for Clarabelle!***

● **FLAP SHOTS!**

PLUS!! OUR SEX KITTEN OF THE MONTH ... WET PUSSY PHOTOSTORY ... AND GUARANTEED! ABSOLUTELY NO BORING BITS ABOUT TRACTION ENGINES OR THE SPITFIRE TO INTERRUPT THE NON-STOP FULL COLOUR ACTION!!!

But when they get home and lock themselves in the lavvy, what do they find? This ....

FULL-COLOUR
PUSSY

Vol. 1, No. 1

CONTENTS

Emma.

BASTARD GAMES ©

Real-life Boardgames

DRUNK DRIVER

'Twas the night before Christmas and nothing was stirring, except you, you pisshead. You've been dragged out of the office party and slung into your car. Now you're on your way home. Try (desperately) to avoid hazard spots, patrol cars and other drunken drivers to get home safely.
DRINK! DRIVING! MORE DRINKING! DENTAL RECORDS! **ONLY £5.99!**

DIPLOMATIC IMMUNITY

You're a Middle Eastern Attaché. Start by smuggling 6kg of uncut heroin in the diplomatic bag to finance your passion for young boys. Proceed to behave as outrageously as possible until you're either deported or become ambassador.
SEX! THRILLS! DRUGS! UNRESTRICTED PARKING! **ONLY £450,000!** *(contains 48 kilos of heroin.)*

ALSO AVAILABLE IN THIS SERIES:
- **RUN, RABBIT, RUN** - SEX! BUSY ROADS! MORE SEX! STEW!
- **TORQUEMADA** - SEX! PERSECUTION! CASTRATION! REAL-LIFE CONFESSIONS FROM YOUR FRIENDS!
- **BENT COPPER** - SEX! MONEY! THE MASONS! GUNS WITH DODGY SAFETY CATCHES!
- **I AM THE JUDGE** - SEX! MONEY! THE MASONS! DEAFNESS WHEN IT COMES TO GUNS WITH DODGY SAFETY CATCHES!
- **AMERICAN PRESIDENT** - SEX! CANCER! STATE TERRORISM! A BUTTON THAT COULD DESTROY THE WHOLE WORLD!
- **PRIME MINISTER** - SEX! ARSE-LICKING! HUMILIATION! U-TURNS!

BASTARD Advertising

Everyone in advertising is an honorary bastard, naturally, but I still think they could take it up a notch:

WELCHING ON YOUR ELECTRICITY BILL?

EITHER YOU PAY FOR IT

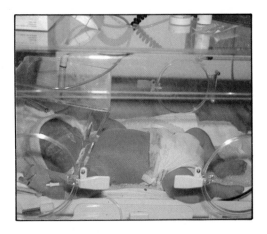

OR KATY DOES...

Don't think we don't mean it. We're utter and total bastards at the Electricity Board and all it takes is a flick of the switch, so you'd better pay up ... for her sake.

ELECTRICITY
We've got the power

BUTTER is the devil's spunk

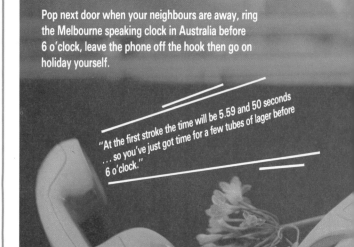

Make someone

Pop next door when your neighbours are away, ring the Melbourne speaking clock in Australia before 6 o'clock, leave the phone off the hook then go on holiday yourself.

"At the first stroke the time will be 5.59 and 50 seconds ... so you've just got time for a few tubes of lager before 6 o'clock."

British Telecom....

A Career with the Boys in Blue?

happy
(us)

IF YOU

CAN READ THIS ADVERT

You're overqualified,
sorry.

The Metropolitan Police.

THE 9 TO 5 BASTARD

07.30	Get woken up by that crappy radio alarm you bought for yourself during the five minutes they were fashionable. Listen to the voice of Mike Smith for about a minute.
07.31	Get your sledgehammer from the garage, go back to your bedroom, smash Mike Smith to pieces and go back to bed.
11.00	Wake up in your own good time, have a leisurely breakfast, put on your ''The boss is a wanker'' T-shirt and wind your way to the station.
12.00	Arrive at the station: read the girlie books in Smiths for an hour.
13.00	1) Arrive at work four hours late and use one of the following excuses – • I got my arm stuck in the cornflakes packet. • I was so pissed when I woke up this morning that I couldn't find the tube station. • Fuck Off! 2) Violently throw your umbrella at the managing director and say, ''Well, you shouldn't look like a hat-stand, then, should you, you stupid bastard!'' 3) Decide it's time for lunch.

Totally BASTARD Things To Do

Number

4

HOW TO CUT SOMEONE'S BALLS OFF WITHOUT THEM NOTICING

''Oh look! Halley's Comet.''

15.30	Arrive back at office having drunk 47 pints of lager and puke in the stationery cupboard.
15.40	Drop trousers, sit on photocopier and run off 200 bum prints.
16.00	Send bum prints to despatch for distribution around office marked "Urgent."
16.15	Make paper dolls from the contents of your in-tray and send them by motorbike courier to Head Office.
16.30	Wave your nob out of the window and repeatedly shout the company's name.
16.45	Erase the last fifty years' sales-ledger accounts on the computer and re-programme it to play "Donkey Kong" instead. Tell the Managing Director what you've just done, and ask if he wants to give you a game.
17.00	Go home for ever.

BASTARD ON THE DOLE

This is brilliant, but only for a short time — unless you enjoy eating dog food and hanging around in libraries to keep warm. Whatever you do, don't let them get you back in an office again. Should you accidentally find yourself faced with a job application form, be careful not to do anything even remotely sensible with it . . .

POST APPLIED FOR: *Stock Controller*

Please complete form in block capitals:

NAME IN FULL: (Only one character per box)

Adrian 'I've got a huge hots' Edmondson

OTHER NAMES BY WHICH YOU ARE KNOWN:

Violent axe murderer of people who take a long time to process official forms.

Try and fit as many letters as you possibly can within the spaces marked 'only one character per box'.

For official use only

Use this bit for warming up your cheap biro, or doodling pictures of what you'd like to do to the person who sent out the form

PRIVATE ADDRESS:

Yes, very private

LENGTH OF RESIDENCE AT THIS ADDRESS: *40 feet*

SEX:

Never under ANY circumstances write 'YES' in this box. Only total and utter twats do this & think it's the funniest thing in the whole world. Instead, just draw a stiffie.

Please include a recent photograph of yourself.

PREVIOUS EMPLOYMENT:

Employer	Official title	Reason for leaving	Outline of main duties
Harry Mad Bastard.	*Safe blagger*	*Near crucifixion when I got a job wrong.*	*Blagging safes, pimping, extortion, hit-man, bouncer, and stock-control.*

REFERENCES:

First Referee
Name: *H.M.Queen*
Status: *Unemployed, but in receipt of state benefits worth £4m p.a.*
Address: *Buckingham Palace*

Second Referee
Name: *Henry 'Fingers' Magee.*
Status: *Entrepreneur*
Address: *Wormwood Scrubs.*

AGE: *912,038,427 seconds and counting*

Send them your old school year picture and say 'I'm in the third row back, fifty-second from the left.'

DO YOU HOLD A CURRENT DRIVER'S LICENCE? *NO, I'm holding a pen!*

WHY DO YOU WANT THIS JOB? *Your building has polished floors, & I'd enjoy sliding along them.*

60

Totally BASTARD **THINGS TO** Do

to Yourself...

1 Move to Ongar

2 Do all your shopping in Woolworths

3 Cut off your nob and post it to yourself marked "*Extremely fragile and crushable and please Mr Post Office Worker, don't even think about jumping up and down on this parcel.*"

4 Ram a red hot poker up your arsehole

5 Have plastic surgery so you look like Nigel Lawson

6 Have a partial lobotomy so you think like Nigel Lawson

7 Appear as a contestant on "The Price Is Right"

8 Eat nothing but All Bran for five months

9 Have a sex change so you can marry John Noakes

10 Blow your life savings following the Nolan Sisters on tour

11 Watch "Delta Force" 152,000 times on the video

12 Watch the "Care Bears" Movie once

13 Go and see the Paul Daniels Magic Show

14 Change your name by deed poll to Arnold Wanker and then try getting extended credit

15 Set yourself on fire as a protest against the £1 coin

16 Dress up in women's clothing and go to watch Millwall at home to Chelsea

17 Have fantasies about Barbara Cartland and the Queen Mother

18 Keep the same underwear on for 52 years

19 Make a date with Samantha Fox and stand her up

20 Make a date with Shirley Williams and keep it

HOW TO BE A euro BASTARD

Let's face it, tourists are vermin and they should all be killed — which is probably why they've got rabies and Spanish air traffic control over there. They're dead easy to spot: they've all got bums and mouths and rucksacks as big as the Northern Hemisphere, brains the size of Jimi Hendrix's pupils and faces like pizzas complete with anchovies; they're constantly blinding you with their dayglo kagouls and they all wear plastic Union Jack hats which hide the fact they haven't washed their hair in so long it's still got afterbirth all over it; they spend most of their time shoplifting in Harrods and asking, "Where's Lye-Cester Sqveer?" and "What is number bus go to Stratford on Avon please thank you?"; and then there are all those nubile Swedish girlies on the tube who give you such a whopping stiffie that you daren't get up and so you end up in crappy Ongar all the time which is absolutely spasmo-ville; and now there's going to be a Channel Tunnel and we're going to have our very own tourist mountain so there's never been a better time to be a Eurobastard and have a little fun with them the next time they bother you in the street, with some really good tips:

- One of London's most popular tourist attractions is a quaint mediaeval village called "Tower Hamlets"
- Ice cream salesmen outside the Planetarium will give you a discount if you show your passport
- The traditional way of greeting a London policeman is to punch him in the bollocks and say "Hah, small penis!"
- London Transport ticket offices double as Bureaux de Change
- Scotland is near Wembley
- Never pay more than 2p for a can of Coke from one of the street vendors in Oxford Street
- All the great tourist attractions of London are within walking distance of Ongar tube
- If you haggle with a taxi driver over your fare he'll take pity on you for being so poor and put you up in his own home, completely free of charge
- All foreign tourists are entitled to one private audience with the Queen per visit to this country. Of course, if all tourists knew this then Her Majesty would be overwhelmed and get jolly tired. So people like me are hired to go round telling select tourists of this incredible offer, and to inform you of the secret sign you have to make to claim your free audience, which is this: simply present yourself to the guardsman at the gate and attempt to stick your nob into his busby (while he's still wearing it).

How to be A Party Bastard

"Crikey, you've got a big one!"

PARTY GAMES for BASTARDS

The Price Is Right

HOW TO PLAY: Each contestant has 30 seconds, using their judgement and knowledge of consumer durables, to find what they think is the most expensive item in the house and hurtle it out of the toilet window.

GAME OF THE AMERICAS

HOW TO PLAY: This is a brilliant game. You are "on" and the prettiest girl at the party has to wriggle on your face until you can name the 17th President of the United States.

PASS THE EX-LAX

HOW TO PLAY: Wrap a 5lb "Suicide" bar of Ex-Lax several times in paper. Sit in a circle and play the game just like "Pass the Parcel". Whoever gets it has to eat it all and thereby forfeit his or her lift home from anybody in their right mind.

Soccer Hooligan Drinking Game

HOW TO PLAY: Get drunk. Sit around in a circle chanting names of football clubs in alphabetical order — Arsenal, Bolton Wanderers, Chelsea, Derby, Everton etc, etc. Then hit each other with broken bottles.

Trivial Pursuit

HOW TO PLAY: If anyone so much as mentions a game of Trivial Pursuit, take the box and shove it up their bum.

THE FRANK **BRUNO**

D A N C E W I T H

A B A S T A R D

! H U C O

R D

I never dance anything except the Frank Bruno, here's how: Find a partner. Come out of your corner fast. Shuffle, feint to the right, left jab to her eye and right uppercut to the jaw. Weave, dodge, back off. Come back with a series of devastating combination punches to the body. Clench. Put your hand up her skirt. (Alright, Frank Bruno doesn't do this, but then he doesn't fight girlies, does he?) Break for the bell, take a swig of punch. Gob it back in the bowl. Start again.

THINGS TO SPIKE THE PUNCH WITH

- Your nob

- Your girlfriend's nob (*I must look into this — is Derek a girl's name anyway?*)

- A 240-volt mains cable

- The Policeman investigating the noise complaints

- The contents of the tropical fish tank

- Your bottom

- Tapeworm eggs

- The Trivial Pursuit game

- A spike

HOW TO PROVE JUST WHAT A *BRILLIANT* SCIENTIST YOU ARE TO ALL THE GIRLIES

You can easily demonstrate your incredibly interesting theory of PERPETUAL MOTION by the following method:

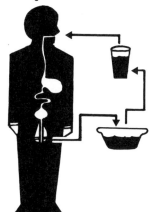

1 Plunge your nob into the punch bowl
2 Start drinking
3 Keep drinking

GOOD PLACES TO BE SICK

- In the punch
- All over the girlie you're dancing with
- On the pile of coats in the spare bedroom (and the couple doing it underneath them)
- Over the coleslaw on the buffet table (who's to know?)
- Over anything of sentimental value to the host
- In the ice-cube compartment of the fridge
- In the toaster (don't stay for breakfast!)
- All over the Trivial Pursuit game and cards
- All the over the person who proposed playing Trivial Pursuit in the first place
- All over someone who's trying desperately hard not to be sick
- Over the head of the driver who gives you a lift home afterwards
- Ongar

Sabotaging the toilets:
THE TURD SHOOT

This is an utterly brilliant trick to play on people and gives you the chance to dress up like a plumber (some people find this a big turn-on, because of all their money and power).

Arrive at a party about an hour early, wearing blue overalls and carrying a bag of tools. Apologise to the host for a) arriving early, and b) coming dressed as a plumber: say you thought it was fancy dress and the theme was 'Vastly Overpaid Jobs'.

Say you need to go to the lavvy and excuse yourself. Once alone in the toilet, set to work with your tools and convert the bowl like the illustration opposite.

I call this the 'Turd Shoot'. As soon as someone does a number two, the water level rises and the turd floats off and down the shoot, straight back into the undies around their ankles. This trick really works best when the victims don't realize what's happened, pull up their pants, and spend the rest of the evening very reluctant to dance.

Now that's what I call getting your own back.

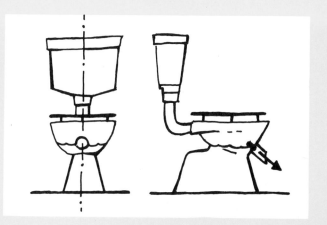

Completely OFFENSIVE Fancy Dress

A·L·I·E·N

Dress up in a black body stocking, wearing flippers, fake "monster" hands and a motorbike tank tied to your head.

Arrive early and crouch down behind the boiler pipes. Halfway through the evening, slowly crawl out from your hiding place, dribbling profusely, and try to tear the head off the girl who looks closest to Sigourney Weaver.

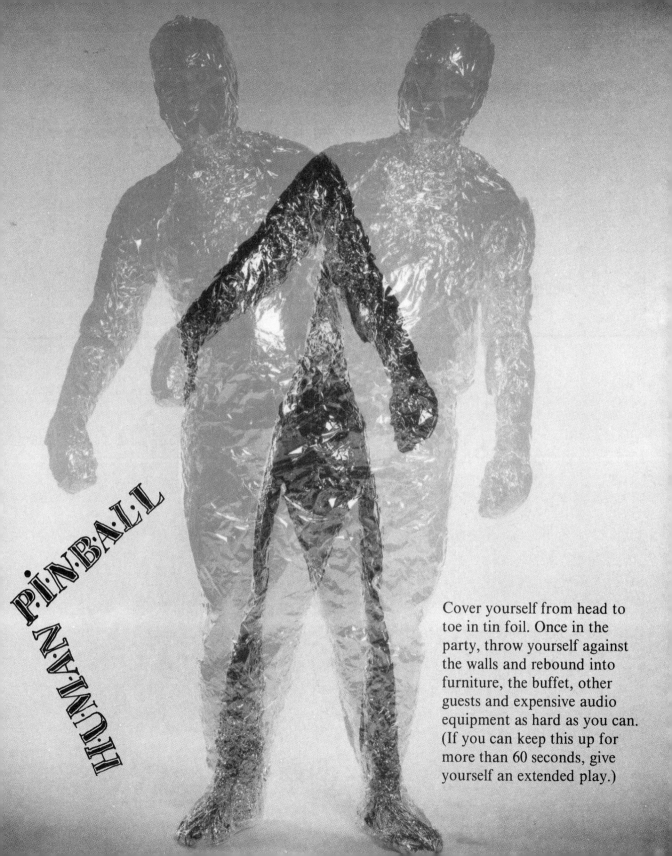

H·U·M·A·N P·I·N·B·A·L·L

Cover yourself from head to toe in tin foil. Once in the party, throw yourself against the walls and rebound into furniture, the buffet, other guests and expensive audio equipment as hard as you can. (If you can keep this up for more than 60 seconds, give yourself an extended play.)

If you are forced to play Trivial Pursuit by some complete arsehole, make sure you slip in a couple of alternative cards:

CARD 1

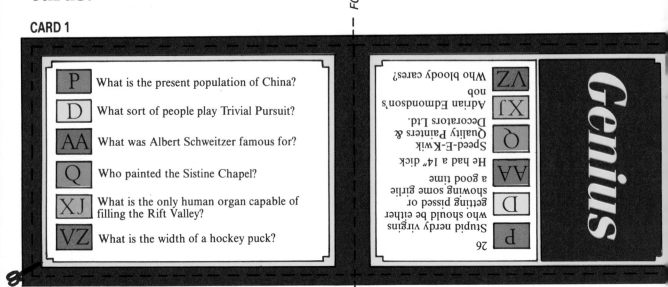

P	What is the present population of China?
D	What sort of people play Trivial Pursuit?
AA	What was Albert Schweitzer famous for?
Q	Who painted the Sistine Chapel?
XJ	What is the only human organ capable of filling the Rift Valley?
VZ	What is the width of a hockey puck?

Genius

26

P	Stupid nerdy virgins who should be either getting pissed or showing some girlie a good time
D	He had a 14" dick
AA	Speed-E-Kwik Quality Painters & Decorators Ltd.
Q	Adrian Edmondson's nob
XJ	
VZ	Who bloody cares?

CUT ALONG DOTTED LINE, FOLD, AND GLUE TOGETHER

CARD 2

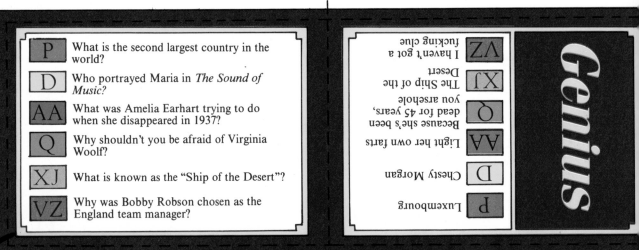

P	What is the second largest country in the world?
D	Who portrayed Maria in *The Sound of Music?*
AA	What was Amelia Earhart trying to do when she disappeared in 1937?
Q	Why shouldn't you be afraid of Virginia Woolf?
XJ	What is known as the "Ship of the Desert"?
VZ	Why was Bobby Robson chosen as the England team manager?

Genius

P	Luxembourg
D	Chesty Morgan
AA	Light her own farts
Q	Because she's been dead for 45 years, you arsehole
XJ	The Ship of the Desert
VZ	I haven't got a fucking clue

CUT ALONG DOTTED LINE, FOLD, AND GLUE TOGETHER

FOLD

ADRIAN "DEGVILLE" EDMONDSON from

Sick Sick Shitbag

PROFILE OF A BASTARD POPSTAR

BORN: A complete prat

SIZE: 2′ 4″ (16′ 8″ in my stacks)

RECORDS: At the moment I hold the world record for looking like a big bogie with a wig on.

LIKES: I would like to understand why anyone would give a turd like me 4p let alone 4 million quid.

DISLIKES: Being called "Tosspot Stupid Hair" by everyone else in the world, including the rest of the band.

AMBITION: To be able to sing or play an instrument.

FUNNIEST EXPERIENCE: A week before I joined the band — which was about a week ago — I was working in a ladies' clothes shop. One day I fell head first into a pair of ladies' tights!!

GRATUITOUS VIOLENCE SECTION

These pages should have killed you instantly, popping up and laying you out, and leaving you in a 'tomato puree' state on the floor.
If you're reading this you'll have spotted something — that's right, it hasn't.
This is probably because you are looking at the book in a shop! And I'm afraid due to legal requirements this page only works under what are known technically as 'Home Conditions', so BUY it and try it there!

If you're reading this at home and it still hasn't worked . . . . . . well . . . er . . . well, that's because . . . oh sod it! You've obviously bought it so who cares? The important thing is that I've got your cash, so *Ha Bloody Ha!!!!* The joke's on you small penis!! (Or if you're a girl — *even smaller penis!!*)

HOW TO BE A BASTARD TO YOUR FRIENDS

72

ADRIAN EDMONDSON, 7 Times World Nob Champion, says:

You Too Could Have A Nob Like Mine!

Let ME SHOW You The Way To A Bigger Nob

Drop your trousers and take a good hard look at yourself. Are you proud of your nob? Are you satisfied to go through life being just "half the man" you could be? It could be much, much bigger. Believe me, I know. I was once "underendowed". People used to laugh at my nob and make fun of me. I was ashamed to strip for sports or shower with other men ... shy of girlies ... afraid of going out on weekends in case I got lucky.

HOW I CHANGED FROM A "MOUSE" TO A MAN!

One day I discovered a secret that changed me from "wee willie winkie" into "the world's most perfectly developed nob" — a "magic formula" that can make your nob so big you need a blood transfusion whenever anyone even *mentions* Joanna Lumley.

MY SECRET BUILDS NOBS FAST!

Just two minutes in the privacy of your own room is all it takes to make your nob swell so big it'll split your pants. No gadgets. No contraptions. No going to the top of the Empire State building, super-glueing an anvil to the end of your nob and throwing it over the side.

DO YOU WANT ...

HELMET ENLARGEMENT?

I can add SOLID INCHES to your helmet, making you feel and look like you've got a German stormtrooper in your pants.

TESTICLE EXPANSION?

You'll see and feel your testicles get so big that they could carry your weekly shopping and everything you might need for a weekend jaunt.

MAGNETIC PERSONALITY?

Learn how to make friends, especially girlies, simply by lassoing them with your nob.

... THEN MAIL THIS *NOW!*

HERE'S THE SIZE OF NOB I WANT:

- ☐ "MUM" ROLL ON DEODORANT
- ☐ CUCUMBER (BUT NOT GREEN)
- ☐ VACUUM CLEANER HOSE
- ☐ LAMP POST
- ☐ NELSON'S COLUMN
- ☐ POST OFFICE TOWER (OPTIONAL
- ☐ CHANNEL TUNNEL   RADIO)

ADRIAN EDMONDSON

I want a big nob. I enclose £100 in cash.
(Big Nobs don't take cheques.)

Name...................... Current Size........

Address ....

....

If I don't get anything in return for my money, not even a reply, I'll be too embarrassed to take you to court or go to 'That's Life' or anything like that. Signed ....

THE INSULT
THAT MADE
A BIG NOB OUT OF "MIDGE"

Best Man

1. THE STAG NIGHT

It doesn't really matter what you do on the actual night as long as the next morning the intended groom wakes up naked, handcuffed to an Orang-Utan, in a cage in the hold of a Boeing 747 which has just landed in Jakarta.

2. THE CEREMONY (fun with the ring)

1. Drop your trousers, pull on a surgical glove and say, "Hold on I put it somewhere for safe keeping."
2. Substitute the ring for one of the following:
   — A Diet Pepsi ring pull
   — A Hula Hoop
   — A Bunion pad
   — A Toilet seat
   — The Rim of a johnny
   — An Oven-ready chicken
   — A Pornographic magazine

3. THE RECEPTION

Make a speech of great charm and poignancy:

"Unaccustomed as I am to making speeches, I'd just like to say a few words about the happy couple. As I was just saying to John in bed the other night, 'I never ever thought you'd get spliced, matey boy — not with a two inch nob like you've got. Who'd have you?' 'Adrian,' he said, 'I know I'm a lucky man. She goes like a rabbit on Dexedrine and she gives great head. What more could a man want, except bigger bristols, but then you can't have everything, and anyway, I've still got Rosie's number if I fancy some meaty whoppers on the side. You know, Jane's never nagged me once during the engagement. Not when I told her I was 'bi'. Not even when I gave her the clap I caught from that salesgirl in Woolworths — course, she didn't know I'd been slipping it to her sister Tracey on the quiet.'

Well, I slapped him on the rump and said I was really jealous. I didn't want John to know that Jane's only marrying him because she's expecting my baby..."

WHEN YOU RUN OUT OF THINGS TO SAY, SIMPLY PULL YOUR TROUSERS OFF AND SIT ON THE WEDDING CAKE.

ALTERNATIVELY:

Club the bride unconscious. Put on her wedding dress and walk down the aisle as if everything was totally normal. Don't give the game away until he pulls back the veil for that little peck on the cheek.

Foreword
A QUIET WORD TO PROSPECTIVE FATHERS
by
Dr Adrian Edmondson BA(stard)

Bloody Hell! Whose idea was it to have a baby, then? Bet it was hers, wasn't it? It always is. Listen matey boy, you don't want one, I promise you. Forget everything Miriam Stoppard says – she's just a girlie, and it's a well-known gynaecological fact that girlies get all soppy and unrealistic and spazzy when it comes to babies. BABIES ARE NOT CUDDLY BUNDLES OF LOVE AND JOY – they're miserable, whiffy and altogether bigger spongers than the monarchy.

So DON'T HAVE A BABY, not in a million billion trillion years or even the amount of time it takes to get through to directory enquiries. Don't. Like you wouldn't put a nest of vipers down your pants, or ask Jackie Onassis about stain removers – DON'T HAVE A BABY!

Just look at the pros and cons:

THINGS BABIES ARE GOOD FOR:

- Filling their pants with shit.

  (That's about it really)

THINGS BABIES ARE NO GOOD FOR:

- Buying a round in the pub
- Bumming a fag from
- Lending you a tenner till Friday
- Wearing to nightclubs to impress the girlies
- Getting from 0–60mph in seven seconds
- Lending you their stash of nudie mags

If you STILL want a baby (like maybe you have brain damage or something), then it's a good job you've bought this book, because I know everything you need to know.

Dr. Adrian Edmondson

Pregnancy & Childbirth

All you need to know about childbirth (unless you're a stupid girlie)

The one redeeming feature of the mess you're getting yourself into is that this is the one and only time when you can get away with drunk driving – "I'm sorry Officer but my wife's having a baby and I've got to get her to the hospital." (Or "jooobgher fur ter boot eyowo a che che hoop a blummener yeoow," as you'll probably say it on the night.) It's perfect! It's fantastic! It's the most brilliant excuse ever! SO MAKE SURE YOU TAKE ADVANTAGE OF IT.

As soon as the pregnancy is confirmed, move all the furniture in the house into one room, and fill the empty rooms with the entire contents of the nearest three off-licences.

Wait patiently for the next nine months. Then as soon as she goes into labour – start drinking as fast as you can.

You should be able to get between 4 and 10 hours' solid drinking in before the contractions get stronger and more frequent and she says something like *"Look for the 400th time Adrian I'm not joking, get me to the fucking hospital before I ruin the carpet."*

This is the time to get into the car and drive out of control towards the hospital, COMPLETELY PISSED YET TOTALLY IMMUNE FROM POLICE HARASSMENT.

[NB: Try not to make the obvious mistake:

POLICEMAN: Excuse me sir, I have reason to believe that you are completely pissed.
YOU: Jooobgher fur ter boot eyowo a che che hoop a blummener yeoow.
POLICEMAN: What wife?
YOU: ??????

YES! REMEMBER TO MAKE SURE YOUR WIFE IS IN THE CAR!!]

By the time you get to the hospital you'll be so paralytic that you can quite rightly demand a wheelchair.

Then immediately on entering the labour room make a beeline for the gas and air, and hopefully you'll be comatose for the whole messy business.

REALLY GOOD NAMES TO CALL YOUR KIDS:

Naming your child is a great responsibility and also a great opportunity for the bastard – imagine the effect you could have on the world if, instead of calling your child something normal, you called it 'Pile Of Shit':

● If Herr Jellinek's daughter had been called 'Pile Of Shit' instead of 'Mercedes', we'd all be saying, "That's a nice 500SL Pile Of Shit you've got there," or, "Can I have a ride in your new Pile Of Shit, please?"

● The industrial revolution could have been sparked off by the Spinning Pile Of Shit instead of the Spinning Jenny.

● We could all be putting Rubber Piles Of Shit on the ends of our nobs instead of Rubber Johnnies.

● Or eating Pile Of Shit Margarine instead of Flora.

EXTRA BASTARD OPTION FOR THE CHRISTENING
"I christen this baby 'I am the vicar and I am a big girlie prat and what I really want to do is give one of the choirboys my special erotic raspberry puree treatment behind the cloisters, Edmondson.'"

Handling Baby

Babies are whiffy and dirty and eject things in every direction, often simultaneously. Handle them with extreme care:

WRONG ✗   **RIGHT** ✓

WHAT TO DO IF BABY CRIES

Put on an Iron Maiden album

Listen to it at full volume

HOW TO STOP BABIES WHIFFING OUT THE HOUSE

Peg them on the clothes line

NAPPIES

Nappies are a nuisance and an unnecessary expense. Have your baby fitted with a septic tank that only needs emptying once a month.

78

Teaching Your Child To Talk

is can be really time-consuming and monotonous
d, anyway, babies have absolutely nothing of
erest to say even when they can talk. They don't
ow who's going to win the 2.15 at Doncaster, can't
imate Spurs' chances next season and don't know
y girls you can go out with. So, to make it more
interesting, talk to them constantly out of a Berlitz
Serbo-Croatian phrase-book.

Point to an object and say, "*Where is the nearest
public library, please*" in Serbo-Croatian, until baby
thinks that's what it's called.

**ima sledeci vlak za
grad?**
en is the next train to
grade?

Muva je u mojoj supi.
There's a fly in my soup.

**Koja su najjeftinija sedista
na balkonu?**
What are the cheapest
seats in the balcony?

**Ne, ali mogu da odigram
partiju dame.**
No, but I'll give you a game
of draughts.

if this seems too much bother,
ply buy it the *Fido* books.

Little Operation

Goes To Battersea

Other titles include:
- Fido Plays Chicken In
  The Traffic
- Fido Gets Rabies And
  Goes Out Of His
  Fucking Mind
- Fido Eats A Baby
- Fido's Head Drops Off
  For No Reason
  Whatsoever
- Fido Does Biggies
- Fido's Bum Gets
  Infected

JN 'N' GAMES
ITH BABY

EEK-A-BOO

Cuddly
Mr Motorway
Hedgehog

ACTION LEPER
'He really falls apart!'

Drunken Driver Race-Track Set

My Little Pony Abbatoir

How To Be A BASTARD At Your Child's Party

The worst thing about children's parties (apart from the gigantic cash outlay on jelly and oranges) is that the little bastards need someone to entertain them constantly. They're too young just to roll up a big spliff, fail to get off with anyone, and then either sit on the stairs looking world-weary and cynical (and hoping some girlie will take pity on them) or drink until they puke all over the carpet like we adults do. As the proud father, this onerous duty falls on you. The best way to cut the party short and get rid of the little bastards is to play one of the following games:

ADRIAN SAYS

This is just like 'Simon Says', only incredibly more violent and satisfying. Sample 'Adrian Says' lines to really catch the kids out include:

Adrian says 'Throw yourself hard against the wall'

Adrian says 'Put your hands up a girl's skirt'

Adrian says 'Do a big poo in your undies and rub it all around till it's squishy'

Adrian says 'Run upstairs and jump out the bedroom window'

Adrian says 'Push your willie into the birthday cake'

Adrian says 'Put trifle down your underpants'

Adrian says 'Get your coats on and fuck off home'

Or simply hire a professional children's entertainer like Johnny Napalm:

THE "WHO CAN EAT THE MOST THE QUICKEST" GAME

This is a wonderful game. It gives you an excuse to eat lots of kiddie food like banana sandwiches and rabbit-shaped blancmange (which, after all, you've forked out for) without looking like a dildo. Better still, all the brats will gorge themselves until they feel sick and cry for their parents to take them home so you have an excuse to end the party.

MURDER IN THE DARK

This is my favourite game of all because, as soon as you draw the curtains and turn off all the lights and switch the chainsaw on and start hissing, "Come out, come out, little piggies," everyone suddenly wants to go home and you can watch TV in peace.

LITTLE ORPHAN ANNIE

This is a brilliant word game in which you simply find out each of the little brat's names in turn, then pick up a telephone in front of them, dial TIM and say something like:

"Hello, Annie's mum? I am just calling to find out what time you're going to pick up young Annie … What? … The neighbour? … I see … Annie's parents have both been killed in a horrendous multiple car pile up inferno … never had a prayer … trapped, pinned helplessly in the mangled wreckage … dental records … you've phoned the orphanage and they'll be round to collect her in an hour … right … right … no, I'll break it to her …"

Turn to Annie and shake your head slowly and gravely. (Note: this game may not actually get rid of them, but it will probably keep them quiet for the rest of the afternoon.)

JOHNNY NAPALM

Let a genuine crazed, slant-hating Vietnam vet re-create the horrors and atrocities of Vietnam at your childs' party!

Johnny's a good old-fashioned laugh-a-minute entertainer! Just get the kids to say things like, 'I can sniff Charlie: he's out on the wire,' and watch him crap in his fatigues. Scream 'Incoming!' and convulse with laughter as he tries to dig a foxhole in concrete with his teeth!

Johnny vividly re-creates My Lai, Khe Sanh, the Tet Offensive, the night his best friendly slowly bled to death in his arms waiting for a 'Dust Off' and the defoliating of the Ho Chi Min trail, with plenty of live ammo and a barrel of 245T!

Detective Tim

in

'NIGHTMARE in Toyland'

"Turn your light out now, Tim-Tims," said Timmy's daddy. Timmy did as he was told. He waited in the dark until at last his parents' bedsprings began creaking, and then he leapt out of bed and pulled on his magic jim-jams.

Instantly, Timmy became Detective Tim, the world's greatest crimebuster. He closed his eyes, said the words the wise old Latvian toymaker had taught him, and when he opened them again, he was back in Toyland where everything was bright and happy, and all his friends lived.

But something was wrong in Toyland today, for all the toys were crowded together in the main square, muttering.

"What's wrong, chums?" asked Detective Tim.

"Someone has killed Paddington Bear," said Super Ted, "He's lying over there."

Detective Tim looked at Paddington's mangled corpse. Stuffing lay strewn about everywhere and his stupid sou'wester was ripped to shreds. One of his big bright wellies, with his paw still inside, lay some twenty yards from the rest of the body.

Another case for Detective Tim!

"It was the gypsies," he said, confidently.

"But they've gone," replied Kermit, who gave him a funny nod and a wink that Timmy had only seen once before, from someone his mummy had warned him about. "They're squatting in the 100 Acre Wood and trying to organise a peace festival."

"That's jolly well not fair! It's always the gypsies in my books," said Detective Tim.

"Not this time," Kermit muttered, his finger all the way up his nostril.

"Then," said Detective

Tim, "It must be one of the toys ... Let's start with you, Rupert. Where were you when Paddington was ripped to tiny pieces?"

"Down the pub," said Rupert. "Bill Badger and Gregory Guinea Pig will vouch for me. I was legless, but not as legless as Paddington here," and he gave a little snicker that struck Detective Tim as being decidedly sinister.

"Then what about you, Postman Pat?"

But Postman Pat ignored him.

"Postman Pat, I'm talking to you," said Detective Tim, suddenly quite angry, "And I don't think you should be doing that with your black and white cat. He obviously doesn't like it and would probably run away if you hadn't securely sellotaped him to the post-box."

"You mind your own business, git face!" snarled Postman Pat, "or I'll give you a special delivery you won't forget in a hurry. I don't know nothing about what happened to that scummy bear."

"Yeah, mind your own business," said Andy Pandy, smoking a very big cigarette and rolling his eyes like billy-o. "Anything that bastard got, he deserved, right?"

"Language!" chided Detective Tim.

"Up your arsehole," replied Andy Pandy.

Puzzled by his chums' behaviour, Detective Tim decided to go to speak to Garfield who was the biggest grass and squealer in the whole of Toyland. But when he got to Garfield's house he saw the cat's tail hanging limply in the doorway. Someone had strung him up with barbed wire ...

"Oh dear," thought Detective Tim, "Something dashed odd is going on here and no mistake." Why, things hadn't been this grim in Toyland since Snoopy got rabies and killed several My Little Ponies in an uncontrollable frenzy.

When he returned to the square where the toys had gathered, his worst fears were confirmed. The Mr Men had all changed. Now there was Mr Chainsaw and Mr Nosepick and Mr Fartypants and Mr Gratuitous Violence and Mr Conservative Party Agent. Tigger and Sooty were helping Pinky and Perky to pull down the Tufty Club sign on a building and replace it with one saying "Mrs Tiggywinkle's Red Hot Love-a-Rama and Shag Palace".

Detective Tim began to get decidedly alarmed. He saw Winnie the Pooh take off his old red T-shirt and put on women's clothing. The Care Bears had formed themselves into a street gang and one naughty bear was ripping the aerial off Noddy's car to use as a weapon. Not that Noddy minded, he was too busy doing jolly naughty botty pranks with Big Ears for all he was worth, the bell on his little red cap clinking and clanking.

"Jesus Christ Almighty," said Detective Tim, "You all did it! You ALL killed Paddington ... and Garfield."

"You know too much kid," growled Orinoco Womble, brandishing a litter spike at him. "Sure we killed the creep ... and the fat cat as well."

"And you're next, Detective Tim," chuckled one of the Transformer Robots.

"I'm going to transform into a dinosaur and rip your innards out through your nose."

"Why?" gasped Detective Tim.

"Because we're sick of pretending to be cute and lovable," snarled a Wuzzle (Tim wasn't sure which one, because they all looked like complete abortions.) "We wanna be us. We wanna be hateful and spiteful and get pissed and do drugs and have rampant sex like real people."

"And what's more," said Roland Rat, "We hate kids. Tonight we're going to come to life while you're all fast asleep, and bite your faces off. Paddington disagreed, being a nerdy girly wimpo liberal, and was going to warn you, so we iced him. Isn't that right Kevin?" Kevin nodded, cracking his knuckles.

Detective Tim gave a strangled sob and began to run. Suddenly he heard puffing noises behind him. Looking over his shoulder, he saw that all the toys had piled on to Thomas the Tank Engine and were steaming after him, shouting rude words and brandishing knives, chainsaws and pickaxes.

Detective Tim screamed – but it was too late. The shadow of the steam engine loomed over him and he was dragged under the big blue wheels, his spine splintering into 47 separate pieces and his skull popping like an overripe tomato being run over by a steamroller.

All the toys cheered as Detective Tim died a truly horrible death.

"Now, let's get all the other children in the world!!" cried Danger Mouse.

And everybody cheered again.

Timmy awoke and gave a big yawn.

It had all been a horrible dream.

He smiled, jumped out of bed, and skipped along the landing to the bathroom.

He squeezed the toothpaste out carefully onto his brush, gritted his teeth and looked up into the mirror ...

... to see half his face bitten off.

BBC 1

10.30am
Playschool

Yet more trouble as Big Ted hits rock bottom, Little Ted hits the bottle, and Jemima hits Big Ted and pushes him out of the square window.
Story: *'Johnny Mad Bastard Flicks the Vs'*, read by *Lemmy from Motorhead*.

9.00pm
That's Life

(I'd leave this programme exactly as it is; in my opinion there is no way anyone could make it more sexy or trivial)

10.00pm
Question Time

Paul Raymond takes over from Robin Day to ask the question, 'What's the rudest, most saucy, kinky thing you've ever done?'
The panellists are:
Wayne Sleep
Anita Harris & Orville
Bobby Robson
Mary Whitehouse

11.00pm
Hospital Watch

A BBC documentary crew run around causing hilarious accidents and cutting people open just for fun. Let the tears run down your face as Desmond Wilcox has a script, a 16mm camera and a boom operator removed from his oesophagus.

BBC 2

6.50
Open University

6.50 Good Morning Stupid Bastards who should have gone to college when you were eighteen.
7.15 Biology: The woman's body (R)
7.40 Medicine: Young Doctors — after some interesting gynaecological openers, Ric slips on a piece of liver and his brain falls out.
8.05 Geology: How to get your rocks off.
8.30 Pure Maths (with a little bit of sex).
8.55 Health & Efficiency in the Iron Industry.
9.20 Science: Alcohol.
10.10 Popeye Cartoon.
10.35 Nude Geography.
11.00 Biology: Famous people who have colostomy bags. The ins and outs and all the names. Debbie Greenwood — has she got one? Or *is* she one? Tune in and find out.
1.55 Pages from Fiesta and Penthouse.

ITV

6.15am Good Morning, Arseholes

Anne Diamond is accidentally decapitated as Nick Owen does a funny piece about a chainsaw. Joanna Lumley agrees to take over at short notice, she jumps out of bed and rushes to the studio. But guess what? She's in such a hurry that she forgets to put her clothes on. The ratings soar sky high and the TV people decide they're onto a real winner and book her for the rest of her life. They change the name of the programme to 'Good Morning Everybody, my name is Joanna Lumley; can you see my thingies?'

12.00 Weekend World

Brian Walden tries to say 'rectum', 'rear entry', and 'raunchy sex romp'.

1.00pm World of Sport

1.05 Saint & Greavsie talk dirty.
2.40 Under-16 Nude Gymnastics.
3.55 Saint & Greavsie go to the toilet.
4.15 Closedown.

6.30pm Dukes of Hazzard

This week those Duke boys castrate Boss Hogg with a rusty farm implement and run their car over his still twitching willy.

7.30pm Soapy Tit Wank

At last, a sit-com without smutty innuendo — they just get straight down to it!! This week, Raquelle, the nudie french au pair, can't believe her luck when she goes to 'borrow a cup of sugar' from Mr Jones and ends up with his cock in her mouth!

Raquelle .... Miss Saucebucket
Mr Jones .... Richard 'King Dong' Briers
Mr Fartypants ..... Sir John Gielgud
A Piece of Snot ...... June Whitfield

8.30pm Tales of the Totally Predictable

'Soapy Tit Wank'
Exactly like 'Soapy Tit Wank', except in this version Raquelle ends up borrowing a cup of sugar.

10.00pm Nudes At Ten

Presented by Samantha Fox and Anna Ford.

12.05am Night Thoughts

'Masturbation'
With interesting sign language for the deaf, dumb and kinky.

4.30pm Countdown

Gyles Brandreth wears another pullover — this time with an enormous penis design on the front.

6.00pm Film On Four

A La Recherche De Ma Petite Chouxfleur
One of six obscure cinematic masterpieces from the continent celebrating France's poet of the cinema, Jean-Claude Dupont. Bernard is an undistinguished novelist living in post-war Marseilles. His personal inner battle between the politics of existentialism and essentialism is reflected in his physical search for a small cabbage, and leads inexorably to a dénoument of extraordinary irony and justice ... in other words, forget about the subtitles and grainy black-and-white, this is one of those great European Sex Romps!!! I give it a five rating!!!

A Societe Sexuelle de France Production.

The Toy Factory,
The North Pole,
Lapland.

Dear Billy,

Greetings from the North Pole! My helpers and I are working overtime to get all of your wonderful presents ready for Christmas. You're going to get sooooooo much this year because you've been such a good boy and Mummy and Daddy love you so very much.

Let me tell you about just a few of the things you're going to find in your stocking (better borrow one from Russell Grant because it's going to be overflowing this year). You lucky boy!

*A football signed by the whole England World Cup Squad.

*A motor-powered go-kart.

*All the Masters of the Universe toys.

*Complete football kits for every team in the First, Second, Third, Fourth, Scottish Premier, First and Second Divisions and the Gola, Southern, and Vauxhall Opel Leagues.

*A Transformer robot that turns into a full-size nuclear submarine.

*Your own pony.

*A miniature model railway that you can ride round the garden in

*A million toy cowboys and indians.

*A ten-speed BMX with CB radio.

*Your own sandpit and climbing frame.

One great way to liven up the prospect of another dull Christmas is to put up a post box in your street marked 'Santa's Postbox'. All the kids think it's great and start filling it with mail, and all the parents think you've suddenly changed from an outrageously dangerous drunken bastard who frightens the children every time you engage reverse, into a nerdy wimpo liberal with a heart of gold and a dick the size of a peanut — that is, until they start having to explain your replies.

The Toy Factory,
The North Pole,
Lapland.

Dear Peter,

I am not going to bring you any presents this year because you have asthma.

Love

Santa

*A VHS remote-control video with 14-day timer and colour TV.

*An 'A' Team van that you and your friends can pedal round in.

*An AirWolf helicopter that really flies...with you in it!

*Commodore 64 and all the games that go with it.

*Every Marvel comic ever printed.

Don't forget to show this letter to Mummy and Daddy. Tell them that Santa never, ever breaks his promise - a that you love them very much.

Love

Santa

Santa.

Being A BASTARD To KIDS At Christmas

The Toy Factory,
The North Pole,
Lapland.

Dear Jaqueline,

Would you like a new gerbil for Christmas?
Yours is going to die before then.

Love

Santa

Santa.

The Toy Factory,
The North Pole,
Lapland.

Dear Lisa,

My, but you do have bad handwriting! I've just got
your Christmas list and have been trying very
hard to read it. I think you're asking for a nest
of poisonous vipers and both your legs amputated
in your sleep this year. I hope I'm right.

Love

Santa

Santa.

The Toy Factory,
The North Pole,
Lapland.

Dear Sally,

Well, who's been a right little madam, then? Who wouldn't
do the washing up like she was asked to? Or clean out
Fluffy's hutch? You know who, don't you, Sally?
Yes, you do.

Your parents have told me all about it and I'm very
cross with you. I don't think you deserve any presents
at all this year, do you? Well, actually I don't care
what you think because you're not getting any. Nothing.
Not one solitary Mars selection box. Not even a crappy
school jumper from your aunty like last year. Zero.
Nil. Not one iota. Bugger all. Not a sausage. And that's
final.

And it's no use crying. I'm not going to change my
mind, matey.

In fact I'm so cross with you that I might even come
round and take back the presents I gave you last year.
I don't care how much you love dolly; if I feel like it
I'm taking her away from you-and if you try to stop me
you'll get a good hiding and no presents ever again.

I get really furious just thinking about you. In fact
I'm so angry that I'm going to get my reindeer to pooh all
over your rabbit hutch when we fly over your house. Let's
see how Fluffy likes that, shall we? Not much I'll bet.
Ho, ho, ho, in fact, I'm quite partial to rabbit stew so
don't be too surprised if Fluffy isn't there on
Christmas morning.

You're a silly, stupid, ugly little girl and Santa
hates you.

Yours,

Santa

Santa.

Alternatively, volunteer to help out with the neighbourhood Nativity Play — hopefully eliciting the following response in the local press:

REVIEWS

"A far from immaculate conception"

Nativity outrage

**by our resident critic
Jack Dribley**

Outrage in the theatre is nothing new — one thinks of *Oh! Calcutta!* and *The Romans In Britain* — but I predict that they will be eclipsed by the paroxysms of fury expressed by parents of the young performers in the St Mary's Church Sunday School Nativity Play, last Tuesday.

Written and directed by one of the adult helpers, Mr Adrian Edmondson, the show featured two hours of crass, mindless violence and horrific jokes of a gynaecological nature, based very loosely on the Nativity.

Offal

I say 'loosely' advisedly, because one finds it hard to believe that Joseph (Billy Fisher), when told of events, would say, "You lying toe-rag! I'm gonna boot you from here to Haifa." Similarly, I have always pictured the Virgin Birth as an event of supreme grace and tranquillity and so both I and the parents in the first three rows, were extremely

Mr Edmondson with the afterbirth

surprised by the tremendous shower of blood and offal that accompanied the graphic birth scene which owed more to *Alien* than to 'Luke'.

Dinosaur

Maybe I'm being very 'old-fashioned', and have missed the 'point' of this 'modern' production, but I must confess that the significance of depicting the Star of Bethlehem by binding two small children together and suspending them by their feet from the lighting gantry, covered in luminous paint, completely defeats me — as did the introduction of totally new characters; Boy George (Debbie Lindsay) and a large cardboard egg-box dinosaur called Lemmy (Shaun Roberts and Tony Biggins) being just two. I also find it difficult to understand why the three wise men (Bobby Thomas, Jeremy Mengele and David Smith) were portrayed as extremely realistic zombies. Surely it was a slip of the tongue when they said, "We wish to braise the infant?"

Piss off

Parents expecting to hear old familiar carols were disappointed. Instead, Mr Edmondson has composed ten new 'songs' (I use the word 'songs' loosely, because I do not consider *'Let's Piss Off To Egypt'* chanted 104 times constitutes a proper song). To be fair, the calypso, *"Christ is Born, Break Out The Booze"* was quite pleasant however, and I am embarrassed to say that I am still humming the highlight of the shepherds' scene, the uptempo *"Sheep Shaggers' Song (Tuppy-Tuppy-Tup-Tup),"* which was marred only by the Angel Gabriel (Julia Manson) plunging from the precarious lighting gantry on to the sheep (Neil Wilkinson and Julie Nicholas).

Slaughter

The final straw for the distraught parents was, I think, the slaughter of the innocents. Important though this scene is in the story of the Nativity, I don't think it warrants an hour and fifteen minutes of any Nativity play, especially when it descends to prolonged scenes of children ripping their dolls and teddies apart with assorted sharp objects.

(Alright, so it's page 89. I suppose you think you've got an enormous plonker for spotting that one. Well, if you haven't, you soon will have after looking at this picture for more than a couple of seconds!)

SEXY DUMPLINGS!

Sizzling, sexy, saucy, skimpy, spinky, spunky, spanky, Adrian "Sammy" Edmondson sure is stacked sky high. And the super sexy singing songbird with the swinging suckers is all set for scorching chart success with her sexy new single "You Can Stick It Anywhere You Like, Mate". She'd shoot straight to No. 1 if she'd show us her stupendous stumpy stovepipes on the record sleeve!!!
(Here are some other words that start with "S" — Stupid, Slag and Syphilis.)

A GREAT NEW INTERACTIVE FICTION GAME
FROM THE MAKERS OF 'F1-11'

SINK THE BELGRANO

PLAYER LEVEL: Cretin
AVERAGE PLAYING TIME: 30 Seconds

▶ WELCOME, THE TIME IS 21,12 GMT, YOU ARE COMMANDER OF HMS CONQUEROR, STALKING THE ARGENTINIAN CRUISER, *GENERAL BELGRANO*, THROUGH THE ICY WATERS OF THE SOUTH ATLANTIC. SUDDENLY THE ORDER COMES THROUGH FROM CHEQUERS . . . ''SINK THE ARGIE BASTARD, STOP, MOVING OUT OF THE EXCLUSION ZONE IS AN OLD & HIGHLY DANGEROUS SOUTH AMERICAN TRICK, STOP.''

▶ DO YOU WISH TO FIRE TORPEDOES?
No
▶ INCORRECT COMMAND: PLEASE RE-TYPE ENTRY
I do not wish to fire the torpedoes, Matey Boy
▶ CONGRATULATIONS, YOU HAVE JUST SUNK THE BELGRANO
Disregard last order
▶ DO YOU WISH TO FIRE TORPEDOES?
Absolutely not, disarm everything and point this submarine in the opposite direction
▶ CONGRATULATIONS, YOU HAVE JUST SUNK THE BELGRANO.
GOTCHA! GOTCHA! GOTCHA! ARGIE BARGY BASTARD SCUM FILTH!
Disregard last order
▶ DO YOU WISH TO FIRE TORPEDOES?
Look do you realise, you electronic nob-end, that if I fire them, Maggie will win the next
election. Now do you really want that on your conscience you stupid bastard?
▶ CONGRATULATIONS, YOU HAVE JUST SUNK THE BELGRANO.
RULE BRITANNIA, BRITANNIA RULES THE WAVES, UP YOUR JUNTA GALTIERI! SEND IN JOHNNY GURKA, THE
ARGENTINES AREN'T MANLY, THEY'VE JUST LOST PORT STANLEY, LA LA LA LA, LA LA LA LA.
Oh God, alright. What's next?
▶ YOU SEE A LOG BOOK ON THE TABLE, DO YOU WISH TO PICK UP THE LOG BOOK?
Yes, pick up the log book
▶ WHAT LOG BOOK?

(GAME OVER)

PREVIOUS HIGH SCORES

NAME	SCORE
THATCHER M	1

OTHER INTERACTIVE GAMES IN THIS SERIES

ROYAL FAMILY:
You are the Queen. Try to understand what it's like to be an ordinary person. Playing time: 170 – 180 years

FOURTH FORM TEACHER:
It's the last week in term, you're feeling menopausal and that provocative little blonde in 4G is giving you the come-on. Can you elude this
Nabokovian nightmare and keep your name out of the Sunday papers? Playing time: as long as you can stand it

REAL LIFE:
You are a spotty wimpy little nerdy virgin who prefers playing with his computer to playing with himself. Can you grow up? Playing time: indefinite

Buy my great new LP

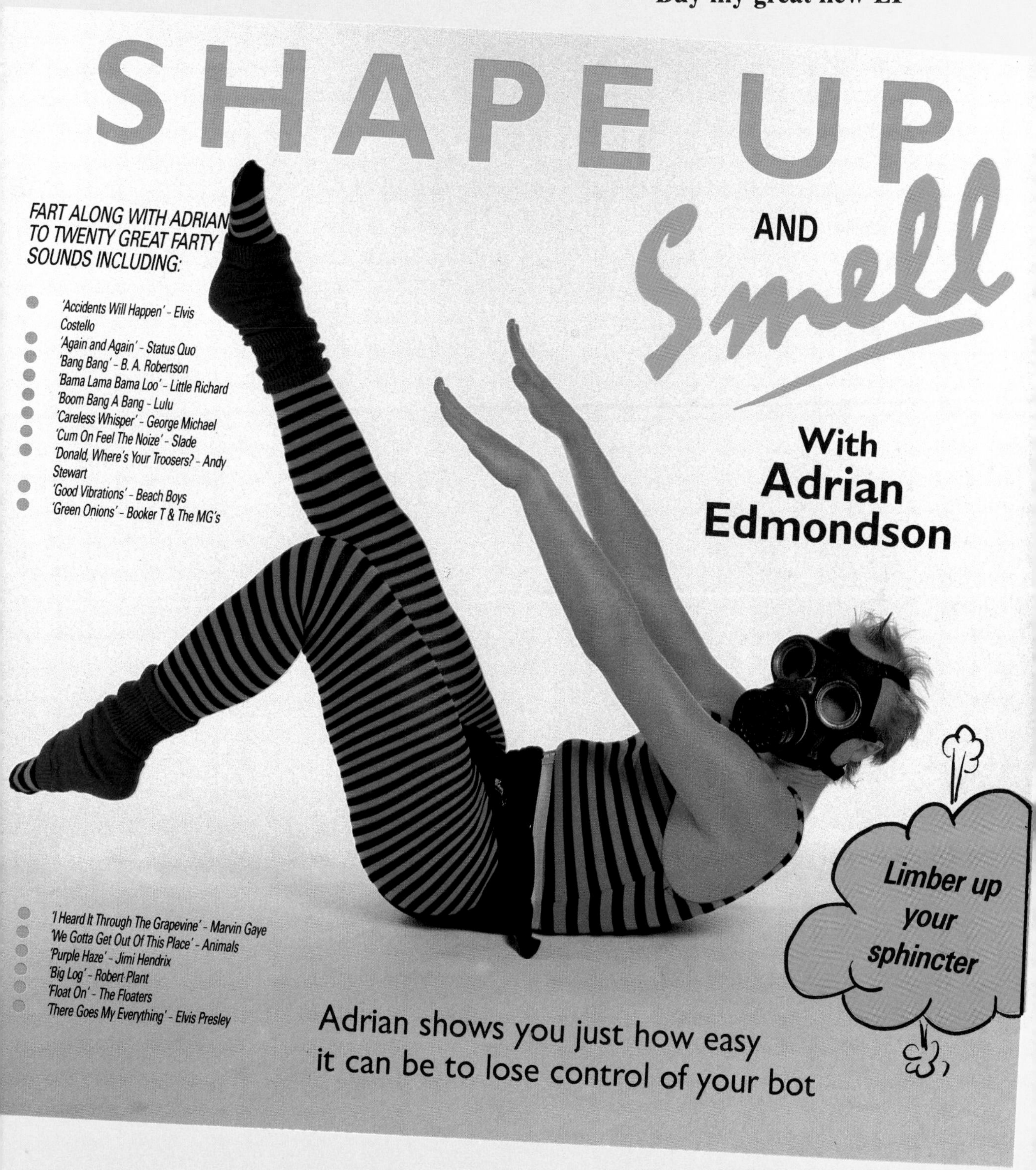

How To Be A BASTARD
at the Chemist Shop...

This is THE place for all your johnny pranks.

1 Blow one up as big as it will go and say, "I'm just checking to see if it will fit!"

2 Ask the assistant to help you on with one.

3

Say, "I'm a virgin and I've never used one before: Is this right?" — and then pull it over your head.

4 Ask if the chemist has a fitting-room.

5 Turn to the assistant and ask if you can have a test drive.

HOW TO PERFORM THE
CANDID CAMERA
TRICK

a) Cut off one of their legs with a chainsaw

b) Set fire to their new car

c) Set fire to them

d) Say you're from "Candid Camera," point to the "hidden film crew," then quickly bugger off the other way

How to Start World War 3 with

I have noticed two things: all world leaders are old men and all world leaders are ferociously addicted to owning very, very, very, very phallic missiles. This has led me to conclude that world leaders must be very insecure about their nobs and to design the following mischievious little trick ...

To play this tasty prank, get together with a trusted confederate (if you're friendly with the great-great-grandson of Robert E. Lee, then so much the better).

Go into two adjoining phone boxes; one of you dials the White House (phone 0101-202-456-1414), and the other calls the Kremlin (phone 155 and ask the operator to get you 010-7095-295-9051) simultaneously. Once you get through the secretaries, the fun really starts:

ME:
(as Ronald Reagan)
Hi Gorbi, this is Ronnie. I'm just checking on the long term effects of the Chernobyl nuclear disaster on your pecker ... Our spy satellites say it's ...

B E E P — B E E P — B E E P — B E E P - **CLUNK**
... shrunk to the size of a raisin.

MR GORBACHOV:
Your cameras lie. My instrument of pleasure is a more respected organ than *Pravda* even! Pah! I will parade it on May Day! Garlanded with flowers ... on two trailers. My admiring people will shower it with freshly cut roses. Mrs Gorbachov, come here, tell this Capitalist miniature-tool-owner just how big it is.

MRS GORBACHOV:
It's big.

MR GORBACHOV:
Thank you darling.

ME:
But it ain't totally and utterly ...

B E E P — B E E P — B E E P — B E E P - **CLUNK**
... as big as mine, you Commie heathen bastard.

MR GORBACHOV:
I tell you. It's huge. The reason we invaded Afghanistan was to make room for it. As I speak, my celebrated glans is brushing the city gates in Kabul, raising the morale of my troops there! I do not need nuclear weapons. I can invade Central Europe any time that I want with my penis! I use Czechoslovakia as a contraceptive! It is huge. It is so enormous that my brain bleeds just to think of it, bastard Reagan. And Chernobyl affected it not at all. In fact it, I personally put out the raging fires with my prolific emissions, didn't I dear?

B E E P — B E E P — B E E P — B E E P - **CLUNK**

MRS GORBACHOV:
It's big.

MR GORBACHOV:
Thank you darling. It is Shakespearian in its breadth, Joycean in its scope and Chekovian in its profundity. When I die, it will be hung in the Moscow State Hall of Art for all to admire and appreciate.

ME:
Well mine's going to the Smithsonian Institute.

MR GORBACHOV:
Listen Reagan. You have two seconds to admit that my organ is superior to yours or I will set about your running dog Capitalist winkie with my SS20s, fascist puny tool bastard Reagan, and you can kiss your shrunken scrotum Dosvidanya.

ME:
Oh yeah ...

B E E P — B E E P — B E E P — B E E P - **CLUNK**
... Try it!

A Bag of 10p Pieces...

MY MATE GAVIN:
(as Gorbachov)
Hello, is that the President speaking?

RONALD REAGAN:
I don't know, I'll just go and check it out ... (Pause) ... Yeah, it's the President.

GAVIN:
Mikhail Gorbachov here. Our intelligence indicates that you have been using Grecian 2000 on your John Thomas to revitalise its pathetic stature.

REAGAN:
Goddamn Commie propaganda! My Ol' Faithful is still twice the size of the Federal Deficit! And that's goddamn blasphemy where I come from Bud, 'cos what I'm carrying in my trousers is nothing less than a miracle. Listen, Ruskie, just 'cos your wife gives me wet dreams, you don't have the right to insult my All-American power-tool.

B E E P — B E E P — B E E P — B E E P - **CLUNK**

GAVIN:
Listen Mr "is-it-in" Reagan, why don't you go back to Hollywood, eh?
Mr Pathetic American B-movie small fry.

REAGAN:
Listen, Mr "seagull-had-a-period-on-my-head" Gorbachov. My penis WAS Hollywood. They made movies on it. *Casablanca* and *The 39 Steps* were shot on location in my vas deferens! I was the reason for Cinemascope. I made Errol Flynn weep!

GAVIN:
I heard it was a comedy short. Ha Ha!

REAGAN:
Well you heard wrong. My "Mr Sausage" is so big that I blot out the light in 30 states of the Union when I get it on. Hell, my wangsnapper IS the 51st state of the Union. It has its own duly elected representatives, state legislature and a thriving industrial base. They don't call me Ronnie "Use The Appalachians For A Tit Roll" Reagan for nothing. When I throb, America listens. When I want to give Nancy her wifely dues, I have to hang lights off it to warn aircraft! If I flicked my banner: whammo! I'd flatten Russia with it! Splat! 200 million goddamn Commies wiped out by a God-fearing All-American tonk.

GAVIN:
In my country, we laugh at your penis openly in the street.

B E E P — B E E P — B E E P — B E E P - **CLUNK**

REAGAN:
Is that so? Well let me tell you son, you got yourself two seconds to admit I've got the biggest willie wonker in the Superpowers or I'll blow your goddamn heathen Commie ass halfway to Pluto.

GAVIN:
Try it, Comrade. *NOW PUT THE TWO PHONES TOGETHER, KEEP FEEDING IN THE 10p's AND WAIT FOUR MINUTES ...*

Absolutely no thanks whatsoever AT ALL go to:

Christy Campbell, Mike Campbell, John Card at Robot Shoes, Serena Cowell, Alan Craig, Angie Crowe, Harrie Green, Graham Hart, Keith Janssens, Mona Kalbande, Stephen King, Jill Kirkham, Richard Kirkham, Ashley Kopitko, Noodle Kot, Melanie Moon, Ben O'Dwyer, Betty Rawkins, Paul Rider, Rowland Rivron, Mike Roberts, Sue Sian, Fiona Tillett, Ed Torpey, Perry and Derek in The White Horse, Beverley Woods . . .

. . . None of whom I know (except for the ones that owe me money) and I don't like them anyway.

My very especial thanks however go to:
Colonel Gadaffy
Margaret Thatcher
Kurt Waldheim
and
Kenny Everett
who inspired me to write the book.

And most of all, my biggest thanks go to me, because I'm Bloody Great aren't I! – and don't forget girlies, I've got an enormous nob! Love and kisses (a punch in the bollocks if you're a boy),

Sexy Adey

Picture credits:
All photos by Paul Rider
except:
Baby: Ace Photo Agency/Mug Shots, **Baby in incubator:** Adams Picture Library, **Colonel Gadaffy:** The Photo Source, **Esther Rantzen:** Adams Picture Library, **Fergie:** Alpha/Jim Bennett, **Girlies:** Ace Photo Agency/Paul Steel/Andrew Conway, Adams Picture Library, **Gorbachov:** The Research House, **Grand Hotel:** Barnaby's Picture Library, **Leon Brittan:** Keystone Press Agency, **Pussies:** Peter Rawkins, **Reagan:** U.S. DoD, **Tom Jones:** Barnaby's Picture Library.

Photographic printing by Mike Campbell.
Front cover photo by Andy Knight.

Artwork by:
Christy Campbell, Ainslie MacLeod, Gerry Malone, Sue Rawkins.